OOK AFTER THE BAIRNS"

"LOOK AFTER THE BAIRNS"

A Childhood in East Lothian

Patrick McVeigh

ISIS
LARGE PRINT
Oxford

First published in Great Britain 1999
by Tuckwell Press

Published in Large Print 2002 by ISIS Publishing Ltd,
7 Centremead, Osney Mead, Oxford OX2 0ES
by arrangement with Tuckwell Press

British Library Cataloguing in Publication Data
McVeigh, Patrick
  "Look after the bairns" : a childhood in East Lothian. -
  Large print ed.
  1.McVeigh, Patrick - Childhood and youth 2.Large type
  books 3.Longniddry (Scotland) - Social life and customs -
  20th century
  I.Title
  941.3'6'083'092

ISBN 0-7531-9750-2 (hb)
ISBN 0-7531-9751-0 (pb)

Printed and bound by Antony Rowe, Chippenham

CONTENTS

FOREWORD

I was born and spent my childhood in a village in Scotland, not very far from Edinburgh. It was not an exceptionally pretty village, but it was at the same time by no means unattractively situated, in the broad and fertile stretch of land which runs beneath the Lammermoor hills and along the shores of the Firth of Forth.

As a hamlet, Longniddry was old enough; the reformer Wishart had preached there in the sixteenth century. The centre of the village, which consisted of a long row of houses with a shorter row at right angles to it and which contained a shop, the post office and the blacksmith's forge, dated only from the first part of the nineteenth century. It was then that Longniddry became truly a village.

After the First World War, Longniddry really started to spread. The railway station, and later the bus route, ensured that it could easily be reached from Edinburgh, and between the old village and the sea, which was little over half a mile away, new and usually quite large houses for the Edinburgh middle classes were built in considerable numbers. Just about this time a "colony" of houses was constructed by a war charity, to house badly wounded and disabled men, and it was in one of these houses that I was born.

Longniddry was situated in the parish of Gladsmuir, and the parish church was therefore more than three miles distant. Gladsmuir (a "glad" or "gled" is old Scots for a hawk) was at one time a much more important village, and thus the church at Longniddry was of recent date, of spartan design and serviced shortly after my arrival in this world by an assistant minster.

Since Longniddry was the biggest village in the parish, the school had been built there, and to this school the parish children walked daily. Some came from as much as four miles distant, for in those days there were far more people living on the surrounding farms, each a hamlet in itself, than there are now. To me, these sixty-odd years seem but a short time away, but in reality today's world is vastly different in such a village.

More than the physical aspects such as the arrival of the motor car, at least in any significant numbers, or the wireless and television, the important fact is that the largely self-contained village community, based around the life of the surrounding farms and geared to the crops and the changing seasons, has all but vanished. Most of the poverty has gone also. Of course there is poverty today, but it is of a different kind — the lack of a television set or the worry of paying an electricity bill. Our poverty was slow, grinding and constant, the kind of quiet despair which never left the thoughts of parents, and especially of mothers, trying to bring up what were usually much larger families than today's on incomes which by any standards were minute and often hazardous as well.

Ours was the poverty of lack of food, of a want of proper clothing (the winter overcoat and a sound pair of boots were rare luxuries), of wet and frozen feet and never enough blankets for the cold winter nights. Lousiness was common, as were ragged clothing and bodies which smelled from lack of soap and water. It is not an easy thing to keep five or six children clean with cold water from the well and never enough money for soap to wash either bodies or clothes; only the most devoted and the strongest of mothers could keep abreast of the battle.

For us children in the village, everyday life had yet another dimension, for the awful detritus of the recently concluded World War was all around us, with the mutilated bodies of its victims in the ex-servicemen's colony, some indeed of whom were our own fathers.

Children, however, seldom worry for long; the world is too fascinating a place. Our particular world was a paradise for children, with the sea, the rocks with their pools, the woods and fields all around us, and safe roads and lanes on which the horse-drawn farm cart was a much more familiar sight than the motor car.

It has all gone now; the farms are mechanised, few people work on the land, and when they do, it is largely with machines. The blacksmith has gone, and who would hear the sound of his hammer anyway in the noise of traffic through the village street? In the smiddy's place is a fancy restaurant with Italian waiters selling second-rate copies of trattoria food at enhanced prices. Where once the horses stood to be shoed and where once the bellows roared to set the fire in the forge dancing, there are carpeted floors, low lights and fake beams.

Where once we picked fruit in long rows or weeded leeks for thruppence an hour, there are now rows of little semi-detached boxes, each with a mortgaged value many times more than the original land of the farm. Our village and the kind of life we led have gone for ever. It is with their memory, now in old age but through the eyes of a child, that I have written this book.

CHAPTER
ONE

The Death of
my Father

The day my father died we had some cold sausages in a pan. I can clearly remember them lying in the big flat iron frying-pan at the side of the grate, black-polished and with a bright steel rail and hob and the dead embers of the fire which normally burned summer and winter and day and night.

My mother had gone alone the ten miles or so to the hospital in a hired car, arranged by the local policeman, I think, who had brought the news that my father was dying. I can remember the sausages but I cannot remember the date, or even the season of the year. I could find out the date now, but it is of little consequence and for a four-year-old child the year has no seasons. There were times when the nights became frosty and the sky was red, and when the wind blew we could cover ourselves deep in dead leaves which smelled of the damp earth; that I suppose was autumn. There were days when the snow came down thick and wet and we watched it with our faces pressed on the window-pane. Then there were colder days when the snow drifted across the roads and the fields, or when we slid along the ice and when even the margins of the sea froze, like pale sugar; that would be winter. There were days when the wind blew cold and one could take shelter at the side of a grassy bank, from the sudden cold rain, and then suddenly feel the warmth of the sun; the days when we went in the woods and on the south-facing railway cuttings for violets and primroses to take home to my mother, who was passionately fond of flowers; that was spring. Then there were the long lazy days, the days when the sand at the sea was hot to the touch, when you could look down twenty feet into the water and see the small fish glide; the days that seemed to last for ever, for the sun hardly went down before it was up again, and mothers called their children home at twilight, and fathers went searching with enquiries and shouted threats; that was summer.

Now my father was dead. "Look after the bairns, Ella," he had said, and then he was no more. The big man with the bald head, the leggings and the rough khaki breeches, and the blue canvas belt with which he pretended to punish me when I needed it. His bicycle with the special seat he had made for me so that I could ride in front of him on the bar, that also was no more. My father was now a glass dome with artificial flowers inside and a little marble tablet with his name on it. For a few days this was displayed in the window of a shop in the village, where those who had contributed pennies and sixpences to purchase it could see that

2

their money had not been wasted. I would go and watch it through the window of the shop, and soon that also was no more and my father was gone for ever.

For a time the house was silent even with six of us still inside. There was a living-room downstairs, which meant that here my mother and father had slept and here the children had been born, while at the far end the cooking was done on the big black range. Off this end was a scullery with a stone floor and a sink, and at the end where the double bed lay was a bathroom, with a bath and a water closet crammed into the tiny space. There was no wash-hand basin. I did not know of such things until many years later. My father hung his bike over the bath on two hooks, and bath night involved heating kettles of water at the open range.

Underneath the stairs was a coal-cellar and there were two bedrooms above, a long one for the four girls and a tiny one with a coomb ceiling which sometimes, usually in the winter, was mine. At the top of the stairs was a large cupboard which, as there was no light in it, we called "the dark cupboard". This was big enough for me to walk into, and after father's death I would go there, for here was his A.A. uniform and his leather leggings. I would often sit in the dark and smell the rough khaki and the leather. It was not grief which made me do this; I was too young for grief, but it was a feeling of his presence which somehow gave me pleasure.

When the opportunity offered, my room would be let and a few shillings added to the family budget thereby. Our village boasted a first-class golf course; my father had in fact worked for a time on its construction, and the championship players would bring their own caddies with them. Thus we had a succession of golf caddies in my room and for a time we had a telephone linesman. There were times, in fact, when we put up an entire family in the top two bedrooms of the house. This was one way for a man lucky enough to have the prosperity of steady work to take his family for a cheap seaside holiday, and for us, all crammed into the downstairs living-room, it meant a degree of affluence, albeit coupled with discomfort, for a few weeks.

When I had the room all to myself was a time of bliss. It had a fireplace, although I could never remember when a fire had been lit, but boys soon get warm under the blankets with an overcoat heaped on top. There I could lie and look out of the window into the darkness and wait for the familiar beam of the lighthouse across the water on Inchkeith Island, as the turret revolved with its warning light. Often it was foggy and the light could not be seen, but then the foghorn could be heard across the water, a long low and mournful moan followed by a high and short note. When I grew older, I did most of my reading here, by candle-light or even — in brief bursts of prosperity — by the light of a torch underneath the blankets, and on bright mornings before it was time to get up from bed.

My father was Irish, but Irish of that peculiar obstinate and prickly breed of Protestant Ulstermen. In Ireland they are British and usually of Scots descent. Away from Ireland they are self-consciously Irish and they carry their Irish patriotism like a gauntlet, ever ready to throw as a challenge at the least sign of a slight to their beloved country. In Ireland, it was said, no doubt by exasperated Anglicans, that if you threw a Presbyterian into the river, he would float UP the stream, and I am sure that saying was not without justification.

Even our names were a challenge, as they so often are still today in Ulster. My father had been called William George, for although he might have a surname used by both Catholics and Protestants, his Christian names proclaimed his particular brand of that much-abused faith. None of us was baptised; that practice smelled of Rome, and in any event my father did not believe in joining any organisation or indulging in any practice merely because it was the custom. He maintained that we could all decide on baptism once we were old enough to do so. Thus none of us were inoculated or vaccinated either, to my mother's eternal trepidation and dismay. Also my father, although badly wounded in the war, refused to join the British Legion or to parade or to wear a poppy on Armistice Day, and he regarded those who did as at best mistaken and at worst as crawlers and place-seekers who dishonoured the dead.

So we were all given Irish, or at least what were taken to be Irish, names. Kathleen, the eldest, feckless and with her head stuffed full of cheap notions of romance, was passionately fond of animals and eleven years old when my father died. Norah came next and scarce a year behind, quiet and thoughtful, thorough in everything she did. Slightly more than a year younger than Norah, Mollie was lively, self-confident and immensely strong both in character and in her body. Mollie had been the tomboy until I arrived, for my father so much wanted a son. Almost exactly a year below Mollie was Marion. Strong in body, emotional especially in her attachment to her mother, with wonderful powers of comic mimicry, Marion was destined for a series of hazardous operations due to a mastoid condition, which left her on the hair-trigger of instability.

Last of all, some three years behind Marion, came myself, the longed-for son — small but very strong and wiry, usually cheerful but with a temper which even at this early age I found so frightening that I usually succeeded in keeping it in check.

There was some mystery about my father; he was born in Armagh at Portadown, that unlovely and bigoted little town set in a lovely land, and he had left home, perhaps run away, after working for a spell in the Belfast shipyards. He joined the army but enlisted in an almost entirely Catholic regiment, the much-loved and much-abused Dublin Fusiliers. This was a regiment without status or glamour, the backbone of the old British army. To serve in the "Dubs" as officer or man meant dreary and sometimes dangerous work in unenvied stations. This was my father's lot, in India and in Egypt and, in August of 1914, in France with the first of the "first hundred thousand" in the desperate fighting around Mons. It was at Mons that my father was wounded, sometime in October, and taken prisoner. His wounds were severe, but without the obvious appeal which resulted from a missing arm or leg. He was wounded in the stomach and groin and what were in those days delicately known as the "private parts". It left him a sick man for the rest of his life, but although he was missing one testicle, mercifully for me and my sisters, he was left with the other, which did complete duty for the two; thus does nature in its wisdom provide.

In the prisoner-of-war hospital and the camps my father became a champion and feared darts player. So renowned was he in fact that at the winter fair in Edinburgh after the war, the proprietor of the darts stall would donate two shillings to my father not to play, when he made his annual appearance. Before this gentlemen's agreement was sensibly concluded, my father won many prizes, including a teddy bear, which was of course for me and which, incredibly, survived long enough for me in turn to give it to my first-born.

The other thing my father did when he was a prisoner was to pursue a correspondence started with my mother, a total stranger, whom he never met until his release. My mother (it is curious how the Lowland Scots use the possessive so obsessively — "my mother, my father, my bed, my tea") belonged to the Scottish lower middle classes. These were the kind of people who clung to their position on the social ladder but always aspired to move up a rung. Her people were fruit-merchants on the one side and schoolteachers on the other, and her father was of that pious breed in whom religion and thrift were indivisible, the sect known as the Plymouth Brethren.

7

My grandparents fathered a family of three boys and two girls. The boys all became sanctimonious crooks, and two of them at least did not hesitate to rob their own parents and their sisters. Both the girls were sincere Christians, gentle people whom life kicked in the teeth and who died uncomprehending and puzzled at the wickedness of the world. In that interval their parents had slid from genteel respectability to ruin, due to the twin misfortunes of misplaced trust and the great depression of the 1930s.

My mother and her sister, as a patriotic duty, had both corresponded with prisoners of war. With the inevitability of fate, both were Irishmen and both couples fell in love by post and eventually married. My uncle George Sullivan had been in the navy, and when at the war's end he married my aunt, he became a fireman. He was jolly and I loved him, and I loved my aunt, who was gentle and kind. They had no children of their own, although he had a son by his first wife, who had died.

Every Christmas my aunt sent us from her home in Liverpool a great fruit cake decorated with marzipan and containing at least six threepenny bits. My aunt was without a doubt the world's worst cook and her cakes could have anchored a battleship, but the fruit and marzipan were lavish and the silver threepennies made her gift a thing of unimagined riches. That cake will always remain in my memory as the essence of Christmas.

My father was so badly wounded that, through the Red Cross, he was sent to Switzerland to convalesce, and just before the war's end, by means of an exchange scheme, he was sent home. "Home" to this rootless ex-soldier was a hospital in London, and there my mother went to meet him and soon they were married.

CHAPTER
TWO

The Move to Longniddry

What was a badly wounded ex-serviceman, without skills and knowing only the profession of soldiering, to do to earn a living and provide for a family? My father was given a short course in the up-and-coming career of chauffeur, a skill suitable for the working classes, and for which there surely would be great demand in the new world where the wealthier classes were rapidly discarding their horse-drawn carriages. Theory does not always fit in with practice. Father was Irish and knew no man better than he was. He would cheerfully be led, but he would not be driven. His employer, by accident of fate, might be the man who paid the wages, but a servant-master relationship was a human situation completely beyond my father's powers of conception. An appointment was obtained on an estate in the Scottish Borders. Father was to drive the car, obtained from ex-army surplus, and mother was to do some housework.

The car had seen hard service and proved unreliable. This father explained patiently to his employer, as a colleague and confidant, after each breakdown. One day, thinking that his services were not to be required that day, my father went fishing on the loch adjoining the house. Sadly, he had been misinformed and, while his employer tried to attract his attention from the shore, father assured him from the distance of the boat that it was indeed a fine day and that he was enjoying what fishing the loch offered.

It was during these brief but stormy months that my eldest sister was born and it was by great good fortune that, soon after the parting of the ways when father's career as a chauffeur ended so abruptly, he was awarded the tenancy of one of the houses recently constructed by the Earl Haig Fund for disabled ex-servicemen, at Longniddry where the rest of the family were to be born.

Several jobs and spells of unemployment followed, although my father was never unoccupied. He might not be suited to work for a master, but by God he could work for himself. He constructed a beautiful yet practical garden within a short time. He scoured the seashore for driftwood and he built two houses for hens, and a rose-bower. At the front door he had two upturned smoke-boxes from old locomotives, scrounged from God knows where, which he used to plant roses in. Since the land at the back of our house was as yet unused for building, father enlarged his garden almost to the size of a croft, by the simple expedient of fencing off a goodly part and putting about sixty hens on it.

Thus we survived and commenced our regular enlargement as a family until, by virtue of his army service, his mechanical skills and my mother's ability to write a good letter of application, father was appointed to his ultimate position in life, as a patrolman with the Automobile Association.

Mother, God help her, was a believer in providence, and used to relate how "they" had written father's letter of application to the A.A. but had no money for a stamp. Borrowing was out of the question, and as mother pondered on the problem she fed the last scraps of Auntie Annie's Christmas cake to the hens. Lo and behold, there was a threepenny piece in the remains and so a stamp was bought; thus the letter was sent and thus father got the job. Mother always instanced this as proof of God's goodness. Like the punter who only remembers his winning bets, mother tended to forget the many occasions when God failed to answer her prayers.

Those were the good years. The work was hard and involved cycling on patrol in all weathers, but there was a regular income, there were the hens and the spuds in the garden. There was also Mr Murphy, a bosom pal, legless in a wheel chair, who disgusted my mother because he swore like the trooper he used to be, and then, within a couple of years, there was me.

What I can remember of my father in between the time I could walk and talk and the time he died is often very clear. I can remember him coming in tired at night and me creeping down the staircase, either to be chased up again or given a hug and a song. "Paddy you're a villain," he would sing, "Paddy you're a villain, Paddy you're a rogue, There's nothing in you Irish, Except your name and Brogue, You're killing me by inches, you know I am your slave, But when I'm dead upon my soul, I'll dance upon your grave," or "There's a dear little plant that grows on this isle, 'twas St Patrick himself sure that set it." "The dear little shamrock"; I remember the words to this day. He would take me on long walks through the woods, and once I remember that I shit myself and he got the girls to stand me in a basin of water and wash me down when we got home. He built a special seat on his bike and sometimes he even took me out on patrol. Then he would cycle to the next village, where there was a pub. There was no pub in our village, for the laird objected to the idea, although the upper classes could drink at the golf club. I would then mind father's bike while he nipped in for what, for me, never proved to be a quick drink.

Several times, father would have got the sack if it had not been for mother's special pleading, and once at least because of her quick thinking. Part of the patrolman's kit in those days of almost empty roads were two large red flags, each emblazoned with large letters in black "AA", to be used at the scene of an emergency. One day father got wind that the inspector was coming, and he remembered that somewhere or other he had left his flags, and they were now lost. "God save all here," he thought: what was to be done? It was the sack this time. Mother had been a keen swimmer when she was single, and she had a voluminous bright red bathing costume. While father cut two sticks from the garden, she quickly cut up the costume and drew the double "A" on the two red flags she had made. Both passed muster in the kit inspection, and the day was saved once more.

CHAPTER
THREE

The Mendicants

Father and mother were both immensely kind people, sharing an almost overwhelming sense of compassion for the human race. No beggar, and God knows there were plenty of them, was ever turned away from our house. Even after father died, mother brought the beggars in off the street to give them a wad of bread and jam and to fill the can (which they all carried) with strong tea. There was no money to give, of course, and indeed none was expected. The beggars used to sit on the stairs, for they were universally lousy. Lousiness was nothing strange to us, although body lice were much less tolerated than head lice, against which mother waged a constant battle, for we picked them up continuously at school. The beggars however were "jumpin'", to use the graphic and accurate term we all employed to denote someone who was really infested, as distinct from the odd and tolerated guest.

So the beggars with their bread and their tea sat on the stairs, and I had to squeeze past them on my way down or up. The memory of their smell remains with me to this day, as does that of so many familiar and expected odours associated with our class: wet soap suds, paraffin oil and children who always smelled of stale urine.

For a very few beggars who were on mother's regular list, there was always a halfpenny; a "maek" or a "bawbee", as that coin was more often called. Sometimes it would be the only coin in the house, but it was still given to these minuscule pensioners. The most frequent of these we all called the "Nail Nail man". This was an ancient and dejected creature in a ragged greatcoat, who came round the doors singing. The tunes were recognisable, for they were familiar hymn tunes such as "Abide with me", but the only words which were ever employed consisted of the refrain "Nail Nail Nail Nail" which, with suitable pauses, was made to fit every line.

My father's humanity was extended to animals, and to dogs in particular. While mother did not particularly like animals and declared that she would not like to own one but would never see one suffer, father was continually picking up stray dogs on his patrol. He would bring these brutes home, and they were invariably large, wet, muddy and flea-infested. "Just for a day or so, Ella, until we discover who owns him", so that the house never seemed to be without the smell of wet dog and trails of paw marks.

Eventually after father died we did have, in addition to Kathleen's pet rabbits, a cat called Tinker who had a surviving daughter, whom she loathed, called Topsy. Tinker, who was a tortoiseshell cat, took to climbing on the roof and warming her bum by sitting on the rim of the living-room chimney, where she became happily kippered. One day I observed her at her usual station and then she was no more to be found. I concluded that she had slipped and fallen down the chimney and, in the essentially practical manner of small boys, accepted her demise. Tinker's fate may have been less spectacular, but she was never seen again.

Animals, indeed, were a much more familiar part of our life than they are even to country people today. The horse was still much more common than the motorcar, and the baker, the drysalter, and even a mobile chip shop, were all horse-drawn. The farm wagons were all pulled by draught horses, great Belgians or Shires or Clydesdales, and farm animals — cattle and sheep — were driven in herds along the road through the village to the railway siding. On the farms, the tractor had scarce made an appearance and the ploughing, the harrowing and the reaping were all done with teams of horses.

Coarse and inarticulate farm boys, the butt of every venomous schoolteacher for their total inability to speak English, became transformed when they sat on the seat of a reaping machine or held the reins of a pair of horses at the plough. This was their delight; then they became kings, and the misery and humiliation of school were forgotten.

My father ran his garden both for delight and profit. Once he borrowed a well-known cockerel from a bosom friend of his (father knew only close friends), who had a coal delivery round. The cockerel, its duty done and no doubt exhausted but happy with the services it had rendered, was put in a sack and placed on the back of the coal lorry while father and the coalman exchanged essential gossip. I watched entranced as the sack suddenly bounded off the back of the lorry and ran down the village street.

There was a very large dog in the village called Jock Haborn. This at least was the name given to that animal, as its master bore the name and had neglected to give any title to his dog. Jock Haborn had a brown curly coat and the most mournful wail. He was silent all week until the church bells started on Sunday morning. He would then stand on the village green and, with his muzzle in the air, he would give his own sustained, doleful wail as an accompaniment to the bells. At this time Jock's master would as a rule be lying drunk in bed, if he indeed had a bed in the tumbled ruin of a cottage he inhabited by himself. Jock Haborn was the village odd-job man and the village drunk, the latter distinction achieved not without keen competition. Since he drank any money that he made as he made it, he could only find work on a casual basis, but his skill with the scythe was legendary and small boys would gather to watch him at work enthralled. Jock could cut the village green to a close crop and, besides, the tales of lost pennies thus exposed were an additional incitement.

It was in a sense through the church that my father was to die, or at least through the church in the person of the local minister, like all ministers in villages of that time still a very great power within the parish. Father did not go to church although he considered himself a good Christian, and this indeed he was. However, like all corrugated iron Presbyterians, he regarded the

18

Established Church, in this case the Church of Scotland, with some degree of suspicion. In addition to this it was, as I have said, a violation of his principles to join anything. Mother did not go to church except on special occasions as, being in the Plymouth Brethren, she regarded it as "worldly". God knows our village church, which was a modern building, was bare enough but it did have a couple of stained-glass windows and an organ, which no doubt put it on the slippery slope towards bishops, incense and, eventually, Rome.

We children, on the other hand, would join anything and especially the Sunday school, which promised both an annual "trip" and a Christmas party. Indeed, for a few brief but happy weeks, the Salvation Army set up a Sunday school in an old hut in the village and we were promised a cup of tea and a bun, by a lady with a funny English voice, so we went there as well. Discipline could not be commanded there, however, in the same way as by threats from known grown-ups at the church, who wisely split us into small groups against which transgression was all but impossible. At the Salvation Army, once the bribe of tea and the bun had been distributed, foolishly at the start of each meeting, the class of 40 or 50 children of all ages swiftly disintegrated into chaos, and the Army folded its tents and admitted defeat.

The village minister intensely disliked my father and father, who disliked no-one, regarded the minister as a poor thing worthy of some passing pity. In addition to his non-joining of the church, the British Legion and poppy-day parades, my father was an outspoken and convinced socialist. At election time, I can recall him speaking for the Labour candidate on the steps of the village green; the parish council candidate that was, although true to his principles he neither stood as a candidate himself nor joined the Labour Party.

The minister on the other hand was a prominent Tory and a power on the local council, itself dominated by farmers and landed gentry.

A new school was almost complete in the village. It is a fine building, and on the roll of honour inside the main hall the name of the first Dux of the new school is painted in gold, "Norah McVeigh", my own sister.

CHAPTER
FOUR

Survivors

There were about 40 disabled men and their families living in the village in specially built houses for the severely war-wounded. Some were quite unable to work, through multiple injuries, through insanity due to shell shock, or through gassed lungs. It was, in fact, a curious environment for children to grow up in, but we became used to legless and armless men, and some children indeed had them for fathers. "Old" Murphy, who swore so terribly, sat all day in a wheelchair, the legless stumps covered by a rug. One man who tried to make a few coppers giving the boys haircuts had been so badly gassed that he spat continually into a tin mug at his side. Father's friend, the Labour candidate for the parish council, walked in a terrible painful drag with the aid of two sticks but, by will-power alone, he did walk, three miles along the seashore each day and by this means he escaped the imprisonment of a wheelchair. Our neighbour through the wall went mad quite regularly. From a quiet man he was transformed into berserk but feeble rages and the van from the asylum would take him away. Then we could hear his wife weeping on the other side of our kitchen wall. A few men were able to do comparatively light jobs such as civil-service messenger, and one was the part-time postman. There were a couple of blind men, but most of the rest were amputees. Two amputees kept little shops in the village. Our village indeed was oversupplied with little shops with ex-servicemen owners, their high hopes of financial independence, like their little store of capital, now largely faded away.

Two of these shops were adjoining, and in one the owner, driven mad by pain from his wounds perhaps compounded by despair, cut his throat. Such was my father's feeling about a man who would seek the easy way out that we were forbidden to spend our Saturday halfpennies with his widow. This was not because of any animosity against the poor woman on father's part, but simply because we must at all costs support the man next door who had chosen to continue to live.

This man, Mr Watt, had terrible injuries. One arm was completely missing, the other arm had been amputated below the elbow. His face and body were peppered with shrapnel and God knows what other wounds were hidden from sight, but he and his wife managed to run the little sweetshop between them. Mr Watt had taken a course in pottery decoration and opened his shop as a gift shop. "Stump Painted Pottery" the sign said hopefully, faded but still there. Few people had bought, for even pity needs courage at times to face such dreadful mutilation, as he intently painted with a brush stuck in an elastic band on the remains of one arm. A few pieces of old pottery stock remained, but the shop now sold sweets and ice-cream and cheap toys. We children were used to the sight of limbless men, and even inured to the not infrequent suicides or attempts at suicide, usually by bloody razor slashing. To me, Mr Watt's shop was a place of riches and Mr Watt was to be envied, missing limbs or no, when he presided over them.

The rest of the disabled mainly worked in the kind of charity factory set up after the war, where grown men made brushes, or poppies to wear on the 11th of each November. They travelled to Edinburgh each day by train, and every evening this procession of the halt, the maimed and the blind would make its way down from the station to the village. Father scorned grown men who made poppies for a living. It may seem a harsh judgement now, but it was not unmixed with pity, and it was in any event the system which father despised, the charitable handouts which roused his anger. It was true, however, that some of these men at least were crawlers and place-seekers. They had bought security in an insecure world. True, they had paid a terrible price, but for a missing arm or leg they had a house and a job and could still command some pity. So they kept their noses clean and joined the British Legion and paraded on Armistice Day and said "Sir" to all the right people. Above all, they voted Tory and despised their own class who were even poorer than themselves.

Amongst all the disabled men, father was about the only one who tried, and for a time at least managed, to do a job which would have taken all the abilities of a man in first-class health. God knows what pain and misery he suffered with his shattered intestines, riding his bicycle to all places in all weathers. With the new school, however, the opportunity to change this came, for the post of janitor was to be created and for this post, which of course was a council appointment, father was generally considered to be the most deserving applicant.

Privately he was told that he had already got the job, and so sure was he of this that I can remember him helping to carry the furnishing for the first completed classroom, from the old school, through the village and into the new building. I can even recall that I "helped" by carrying a pencil sharpener for him. It was not to be, however; the village minister led the opposition to father's appointment on the council, and an incomer, much less badly disabled that father, was given the job.

Within a few weeks, father was dead. He had heard of a man who wanted to become a member of the A.A. in a village about seven miles away, and one wet and windy evening after work he bicycled to find that man, for each new member was worth five shillings commission, and five shillings was a lot of money to us. Father got pneumonia that night and he was taken to Edenhall hospital, which was a military hospital dealing only with the war wounded. Within a few days he was dead, but officially he had died of causes unconnected with the war and his small pension died with him. My mother's total income was now twenty-seven shillings a week widow's pension, which worked out at five shillings for the eldest child, three shillings each for the others, and ten shillings for mother.

If, in fact, the family income had been as much as twenty-seven shillings then mother, by virtue of the weekly miracle she seemed to perform, might just have managed to feed us. The picture was in fact a much bleaker one, for the rent of the house, which at all costs must be paid, was ten shillings a week, or more than a third of the total income. With father gone, the hens soon went and the garden became neglected. There was no one now to arrange these invaluable supplements or to make the economies obtained once by father, who cut the children's hair with his big clippers and who soled all our boots in the evenings, sitting with a mouthful of nails and his cobbler's last between his knees.

All of us, with the exception, for a time at least, of myself, had to think of getting work of some sort, and work of various sorts there was indeed to be had. Mother was the first to get a job. The old school was still functioning and for about a year, until it was finally closed, she went up at seven each morning to light the fires in the iron stoves which were in each classroom and to sweep the floors. These stoves were always lit, except for a few of the hottest days in summer.

Many of the children walked to school from outlying farms, some as far as four miles away. Tiny children of five and upwards had a daily walk of up to eight miles in all, and on days when it rained they arrived at school soaking wet. In winter their feet were of course sodden. Few could afford wellington boots and many had broken footwear with ragged holes in the toes. The stoves were used in an attempt to dry out some at least of the children's clothes during the day. Additionally, every child from the farms, those who could not get home to dinner (we had never heard of lunch), carried a box with a piece of bread and jam and a tin bottle which held cold tea. The bottles were heated on the top of the stoves and this tea with the wad of bread, often without butter, sustained the children during the mid-day break. School meals or school milk were luxuries then unthought of, although within a few years, due no doubt to milk surpluses, a scheme of payment for hot malted milk was introduced at the new school.

Under such ferocious conditions it was inevitable that many children, especially from outlying farms and from the poorest homes, went to school only intermittently. Some parents had not the heart to send tiny children along muddy and rain-soaked roads; some children lacked shoes at times, and small boys came to school with the flesh showing blue through the ragged backside of their trousers. Bigger children were often kept off school when extra work came along on the farm, and with it some extra money; most farm boys hated school anyway, so they often played truant on fine days to go off and snare or ferret rabbits.

The school attendance officer therefore was a busy and familiar figure and, like the local "polis", he went his rounds on a bicycle. Like the policeman, too, his movements were well monitored, and since his coming was known in advance, his enquiries were often met with a closed door or an assumed ignorance, the common defence of the poor when they are spied upon or interrogated by officials.

Mother was paid three pence an hour for her work, and she also did some rough housework in the headmaster's house adjoining. The incumbent of that house, a retired head teacher, complained often and bitterly that mother used too many sticks to light his fire and that, as an ex-boy-scout, he knew she needed a maximum of four.

During this time, when mother went to work in the mornings and the girls were at school, she had no choice but to leave me in the house, usually still in bed, until she returned. I can recall one such morning when she had left me thus with a breakfast which included a scrambled egg in a cup. The coalman happened to call on his rounds on that particular day. Failing to get any response to his knock, he peered through the window and seeing his blackened face, I took fright and threw the egg cup at him which cracked the window pane

There were opportunities too for the girls, in the shape of delivering milk from the local dairy. There was in fact no dairy in the village, but from three or four miles distant a van called each morning and set up a sort of depot outside one of our shops. Longniddry was expanding rapidly, partly with working-class houses but in the main with bungalows for the middle classes who found it convenient to travel daily to and from Edinburgh, with the attractions of the sea and a good golf course to hand.

I speak now of the days before the introduction of that familiar receptacle, the milk bottle. These would make their appearance, in fact, just about the time I inherited my share of the milk round, but before this every household had several milk cans, usually a quart size, a pint and a small one for cream. The milk was delivered by each girl, who carried a massive oaken yoke which fitted on the neck and was supported on the back. From this yoke hung the churns and a funnel was carried in the hand. In this way the two eldest, Kathleen and Norah, children of eleven and ten, respectively, were introduced to the workaday world.

CHAPTER
FIVE

Family Economics

Soon Norah was to graduate to a paper round and an old bicycle and Mollie took up the vacant space on the milk yoke. The paper shop was a kiosk at the railway station, run by yet another disabled man, Mr McAdam, who had an amputated arm. Mr McAdam was a gentleman who took a fatherly interest in the girls as each in turn graduated from milk to newspapers. All of this of course was before school, from six o'clock in the morning, but it yielded as much as two shillings a week to each girl. The paper round was both morning and evening which involved Saturdays also, a distinct disadvantage on a hot summer Saturday, when a day's swimming at the sea had to be called short to meet the four o'clock paper train.

Strangely, my eldest sister Kathleen played only a short part in this saga of odd jobs, because within about a year of my father's death she had left school and home as well, launched early on that almost inevitable career of underprivileged working-class girls at the time — domestic service. On the grounds of hardship, it was then possible for children to obtain exemption from further schooling at the age of twelve, and this exemption was given to Kathleen. The decision was largely a matter of grim mathematics for, with Kathleen taking up full-time employment, mother would lose five shillings a week from her pension. At the same time, Kathleen would earn thirty shillings a month and her keep, although she would have to supply her own uniforms. Mother took the bus to Edinburgh, not for the last time with her wedding ring and her gold watch that father had given her as a wedding present, and Kathleen was kitted out from the pawn money to commence a series of dreary jobs in "service".

I know now that the decision to take Kathleen from school was essential if the rest of the family was to stay together. Mother had been approached by several well-meaning people with the promise that they could get at least several of us into institutions where we would be well looked after. Their chief target was, in fact, me, and considerable pressure was brought to bear on mother to get me into the Queen Victoria School at Dunblane. In this excellent establishment for children of soldiers I would be clad in the kilt and given a first-class education, and no doubt in the material sense I would have done well in the world. I so often thank my gentle but stubborn mother, who must have resisted the most enormous pressures upon her to split her family, which "charity" in those days so often involved.

I was anxious too that I should help in some way. No small boy of course could ever grasp the idea of being poor, or even of money itself. One Christmas — I think it must have been the first or second one after my father died — a parcel was delivered to us through the offices of a tall and gaunt but very kind lady who did charitable visiting. Inside that box, and I remember it so well, was a tin with some ham, an iced cake with a pink and white top and four large well-scrubbed potatoes. "Why", I asked mother "did they send us potatoes?", for we still had a lot in the garden. "Because", she said, "that's what all poor people get." "But we're not poor," I protested, and she smiled her sweet, sad smile.

I would often creep down the stairs at night and see mother softly crying to herself at the fireside. I knew she was crying for my father, and I knew that if she had some money she might be happier, but I was seven before there was any way I could do anything about it. By that time Kathleen was away at yet another of her service jobs. She had come home in tears from the first because the butler had made "advances" to her. Norah was doing the paper round and Mollie and Marion were looking after the milk. On Sundays I was already delivering a few papers, for which I was paid tuppence, and to one lady I delivered a standing order of the *News of the World* and two Abdine powders, the once universal Scottish cure for everything from constipation to a hangover. This lady was wealthy, for she had a son in the Canadian "mounties" who sent her dollars in an envelope. She always gave me a Mars bar and this little perk, which was bequeathed to me by one of my sisters, was carefully tended by me in turn until it was passed over to another boy on my leaving the village.

Somewhere or other there was a law that said no child could have paid employment until the age of ten but, on the legend that I was only helping my sisters, I commenced work at the dairy at one and sixpence a week.

This decision to commence work was precipitated by a financial crisis which for us was of immense dimensions. Norah had moved from the milk round to deliver papers for Mr McAdam who ran his paper stall at the railway station. There was a very wide area to be covered both morning and evening, and a bicycle was essential for the paper job.

The very poor are always trapped into buying dear through lack of money. Had we even had a few shillings we would probably have been able to buy a second-hand bike. As it was, mother had to go up to Edinburgh and agree to buy a new one on hire purchase. The bicycle cost £5.19/6d and was to be paid for at one and sixpence a week, which of course would come out of the money for the paper round.

In theory this was a good idea, but only a couple of weeks after the bicycle was bought, Kathleen borrowed it and rode into the path of a motor cyclist. She was brought home crying and bleeding although not seriously hurt, but the bicycle was a complete wreck. There was no insurance compensation and, although the cycle firm supplied another and well-used machine, it meant that now both the ruined cycle and the second-hand one had to be paid for.

It is difficult today to imagine the despair which such a crisis can cause in a family trapped by the extremes of poverty. Norah had to have another bike, and somehow both had to be paid for. Thus I became a milkman.

My job was in fact an easy one. I met the milk van at six o'clock and, once it had deposited the milk at the depot for my sisters to deliver on foot, the dairyman and myself would look after the more outlying deliveries in the big houses down by the sea.

Milk bottles were just taking over from cans then, and we carried so many of these and several big churns. The bottles were of both quart and pint size with waxed paper stoppers which fitted on the tops. The milk was beautiful, creamy and fresh, and it was unpasteurised. Davie Black was the milkman and he despised the pasteurised milk which the co-operative store was starting to sell in the village. Davie called it "biled shite", which in a sense was not so far off the mark. Davie made a call most mornings at a big house where he said that the cook was his sister. This often took him a quarter of an hour or more, and sometimes I wondered that it did not take me that long to see MY sister, but then I was a seven-year-old and the mysteries of sex had still to be unveiled to me. When Davie ran out of milk bottles on his rounds, he would pick the cleanest looking from those returned at the doorstep and fill them from a churn on the back of the van.

Despite all these jobs, the possibilities of employment had by no means exhausted themselves for the McVeigh family. Ours was a market garden area, and in the season spare hands were always wanted at such jobs as berry-picking and weeding. The hourly rate was the usual threepence, but so far as berry-picking was concerned, this was usually paid by the piece, a halfpenny per pound for such fruits as rasps and currants and of course much less for the easily picked strawberries. Perhaps the earliest recollection of my life is crawling up between the long lines of strawberry plants on the field which bordered the village and gorging myself unobserved.

Working for a wage in the fields, however, was different and closely supervised. With good weather, it was possible to make perhaps sevenpence for two hours' work after school, and during the holidays we could work several weeks at a stretch where rumours of vast sums being earned, as much as fourteen shillings in one week, spurred us on for the short season.

We couldn't pick berries during the rain, but after rain there was always a rush before they would spoil, and we quickly became soaked from the dripping bushes. Protective clothing was unknown to us and we accepted our dripping wet condition as part of the job.

Weeding was an hourly paid job which could be done after school. We were paid each evening, six pennies, and I can recall my feeling of pride in taking these home to mother for the first time. Still in short trousers, my knees became muddy and sore. The workers were supervised by the old father of the farmer

Allen. "Gaga Allen" was reputedly ninety-two years of age and of fearsome reputation. He was lame and walked with the aid of a walking stick in one hand and a golf club in the other. Thus equipped, he patrolled the kneeling rows of workers. One's instinct was to lean with the one hand and to weed with the other, and this I did until I felt the thump of Gaga's walking stick on my backside and heard his voice growling at me. "Yase baith yer haunds", he advised me, and thus I was cured of this pernicious practice and Gaga ensured that he got his full thruppence worth.

We never really exhausted the possibilities of making money. We ran errands, which are always "messages" in Scotland. We hung about the post office on rumours that a telegram was impending to be delivered to one of the outlying farms. The fee for a walk of several miles could range from tuppence to as high as fourpence, and a penny tip was not unknown. We went "Guising" at Hallowe'en, but that tended to be an overcrowded occupation. A few fireworks were let off, by the better-off English in the main (anyone who spoke English was considered to be English), on Guy Fawkes Night. Christmas was mainly for children, and some children still got their presents at New Year. For the adults, New Year and Old Year's Night, Hogmanay, were the real holiday and Christmas was still a working day.

I never graduated to the really backbreaking work of the potato fields, the "tattie howkin" which Norah and Mollie both worked at. This was the highest-paid work, worth fourteen shillings a week and geared to the harvesting machine's speed. I still marvel at how these children of twelve and thirteen could trudge along with bent backs holding the heavy creels for ten hours a day, but before I was big enough to learn this skill, we had left the village.

We gathered brambles in September, both for mother to make the jelly and for a few people willing to pay for the fruit, and I filled a big basket with fresh mushrooms in October for "Daddy" Bell, the engine driver, and the only person we knew in the village who would eat mushrooms and for this I would get tuppence.

When the time came for Norah to leave school, the rector pleaded with mother to let her stay on because she was a brilliant pupil with so much promise. What senseless pleading; surely he should know that the idea of an education one day more than the state demanded was for us an unattainable luxury. When that time came, Norah took a job as a messenger girl for the local fruitmonger.

The Wybers had two shops, one in Edinburgh and one to serve the growing middle-class community in our village. They, husband and wife, were both mean: he was quiet and mean and she was vociferous and mean. For twelve shillings a week Norah cleaned the shop and cycled her rounds with great baskets of vegetables and fruit, and when I became nine years of age, on Saturday morning, which was the busiest part of the week, I helped her. For four hours, which worked out at the inevitable thruppence an hour, I cycled up and down long roads with an ancient machine which was much too big for me and with two baskets, one balanced on either side of the handlebars.

Mrs Wyber, who had a drip constantly on her nose, watched me with gimlet eyes in case I stole the fruit. Our parents had taught us absolute honesty in even the tiniest matters, and stealing of any sort was something which never entered our heads. This of course the Wybers should have known but if they did know, they still would never have believed it. On odd mornings when I had been kept half an hour late, Mrs Wyber would give me an apple with my shilling or even some sweets which had become too stale to sell. Once my bicycle toppled on top of my load and the brake lever pierced a banana. I pulled the banana from this spit and smoothed down the skin and delivered my load. Back at the shop the telephone rang. It was an irate customer complaining about the condition of one banana, and I was immediately despatched several miles with a single replacement.People like the Wybers convinced themselves that they were helping a needy family by employing us. I am quite sure that they looked on this vicious exploitation as an act of charity. They are not wholly to be blamed; in many ways the world of our childhood was a much more callous and uncaring world than our particular corner of the world today.

CHAPTER
SIX

School; The Smiddy

In many ways we were a peculiar family, and one of the marks of our eccentricity was that we all loved school. Even poor Kathleen, whose reading was largely confined to lurid and cheap romantic magazines, liked what little schooling she had. Between the time of father's death and when she was given her exemption certificate, she had to stay off school a great deal to look after us while mother went to work.

We all started school at the old building in the village with its stone walls and tiny concrete playground, and the only heating the stoves where the farm children tried to dry their clothes and warm up their tea cans. The senior pupils were given turns of ringing the cracked handbell which signalled the commencement and finish of lessons and the breaks during the day. We would dawdle by the blacksmith's forge if we were early in the morning, until the bell started its cracked ring, and then we could run to the school yard to form up in the line, within a minute or so.

The blacksmith's was for us a place of endless fascination. He was both a blacksmith and a farrier, so that there were often rival attractions going on at the same time. Our way to school was guided by the ring of the blacksmith's hammer, that sweet musical ring; the strong forging blow followed by the light taps on the anvil to dissipate the heat on the hammer head, while the smith judged the exact place of his next blow. The smith had three sons, each big and strong but patient both with horses and with us children, and each with his big leather apron.

From the shop came the most wonderful smell, compounded of wet coals, of singed horse hooves and of charred wood. The bellows were worked by hand, and while one son pulled up and down on the long handle, the fire would burst into a great flame and give a giant's roar as it leapt awake. One of the other sons or the father would manipulate an iron bar or a ploughshare in the fire until, from the colour, he knew that the heat was just right. Then, with a pair of great tongs, he would swing it onto the anvil.

The most spectacular sight at the forge was when the smiths made new iron tyres for the great cartwheels and then, when they were white hot, carried them out to the yard where they were shrunk onto the wheels by cooling with buckets of water. This required the full complement of father and sons, and often I watched fascinated by their skill and by the clouds of steam from the water, oblivious of the school bell.

Almost as fascinating was the farrier's shop. This had a wooden floor, as opposed to the stone floor of the smithy. The reason for this was of course so that the horses didn't slip, for a horse standing on three legs while being shoed is very vulnerable and a horse which has slipped and fallen is a terrible sight. There was a hill in the centre of our village, and in winter the steep incline in the road was always a hazard for horses, who frequently slipped on the ice which always seemed to collect there. Most survived the fall and were able to get up once the cart shafts had been removed. From time to time, however, a horse broke a leg and had to be shot on the spot. Then it was Mr Gillon who was the home farm grieve and who had a rifle and who, it was said, had been a sniper in the war, who was summoned. Two men would hold a hap (a cover or blanket) up in front of us curious boys and there would be a loud crack. The dead horse would be dragged by a rope by another horse, up into its own cart, and we would stare at the trickle of blood on the frosty ground.

The farmworker who had brought in a horse for shoeing would stand by its head with a short lead. This was a little holiday for him, a chance to come into the village and to have a chat with the smith and to smoke his pipe. The smith would take each hoof in turn between his knees, standing astride the horse's leg and facing towards its rear. This position allowed him to nudge the flanks of the horse with his own thigh, getting it to adjust the position of each hoof much as a barber will incline the head this way and that while he gives a haircut. The horses understood and enjoyed the whole process. Of course in our language the smith never nudged the horse; he "gi'ed him a dunt" and he never pulled out the old nails in the hoof, he "howked" them, which is a much more accurate description in any case.

The old shoes taken off, the smith would then cut and pare the hooves for a clean fit. The new shoes, a particular size for each horse, were then tried one by one while they were still red hot from the forge. Thus the smith could see from the burn marks if they were fitting properly. The shoe was then cooled in water and the nails were driven home, each one driven out towards the surface of the hoof so that it could not work its way in and lame the horse, and with its point then nipped off and filed smooth.

Fascinated though I was by the smiddy, I never had any intention of being a blacksmith when I grew up, but it was the same smiddy that nearly brought death to my sister Norah one day. We all used the little shortcut it afforded on our way home from the sea, and Norah stepped on a large nail here, which pierced her thin gymshoe and went up into her foot. She contracted blood poisoning as a result, and for weeks was in danger of dying.

Doctors were always a worry for mother, for of course she had to pay the fee. There was never any question of the doctor refusing to call, and the village doctor was a good and compassionate man. Still the fee, however small, had to be paid, so we always conspired with mother to put off calling the doctor unless it was vital to do so. Thus Norah did not receive the immediate medical care which might have prevented so dangerous a case of blood poisoning. I recall limping around for weeks myself with a sore foot because of the thought of the doctor's half-crown. Years later I discovered I had broken a bone in my foot. It had knit again, of course, but it still locks itself in a painful position if I hold the foot the wrong way.

The children at school fell into two distinct categories. There were the village children and the farm children. The village children included some from the middle-class villas and bungalows for the first two or three years at school. Once they were about eight years or so old, these children would go off to boarding-school or travel each day to private schools in Edinburgh. Meantime, for the first years of schooling there was an element of democracy, for some of the better-off children at least. It was a spurious democracy, for I cannot recall a single real friendship as a result, and no working-class villager ever entered the house of a middle-class incomer, except as a handyman or a maidservant or charwoman, this last being more familiar to mother in her relations with her better-off neighbours.

The farm children included some from the centre of the village, the oldest houses of which belonged to the home farm. These farms of the Lothians were very large and very rich. Before the rapid mechanisation which followed the prosperity of the war days, they all supported large labour forces, as many as fifteen to twenty families. The farms were in effect small hamlets in themselves and to a very large extent formed self-contained communities, where husbands and sons, and wives and daughters too, worked for the same master.

There was nothing of the romantic tradition of the Scottish "lad o' pairts" amongst the children of these rural proletarians. They had little love of learning and they could not, as fee'd workers and tenants of tied houses, indulge in the luxury of personal opinions or independent thought. They were hired by the year, often by an arrangement which included the labour of their children and wives, and they were miserably underpaid. There were exceptions, of course. The shepherd, who was highly skilled and lived and worked apart, was the aristocrat amongst farmworkers, and the grieve or foreman often had a measure of independence and authority.

The farm workers, "farm-servants" as they were officially described, were almost all itinerant. They hired out for a year at Martinmas or Lammas, and at these times the country schools would close so that families could move from the disappointment and complaints of one "fee", with its poor wage and leaky cottage, to the high hopes of another farm, which inevitably turned out to be as bad or worse after a few months or weeks.

At "term" time whenever we walked along the roads we would come across a cart with its occupants moving from farm to farm. Even as a boy I could feel some pity for the family with all its possessions piled up in the cart, mainly a big double bed or perhaps two, and a kitchen dresser of cheap pine, usually painted green. The few household goods were as many as we had in our own home, but it was the exposure of poverty on the back of a slow-moving cart which I felt, and which I will always remember.

The farm children who came to our school then were mostly poor, as we were of course. They were often verminous and, although they worked on some of the richest land in Britain, they ate white factory bread and margarine and cheap jam and they were often underfed and sickly. Most children in those days had a runny nose both summer and winter, but especially in the cold, called by the graphic Scottish word a "snotter". Most children also had a great mark on their right sleeve, which was their substitute for a handkerchief. Sometimes the more caring and despairing mothers would even sew buttons on this part, so that wiping the nose was painful; then the mark would be transferred to the other sleeve.

We were taught our lessons using slates, and each child was supposed to bring from home a clean rag soaked in fresh water. Usually a large part of the class were without rags, and cleaned their slates by the simple expedient of spitting on them and rubbing the surface with the elbows of their jerseys. Thus elbows too were almost invariably marked or rubbed clean through.

In the old school we sat at long benches which were fixed to the battered desks by an iron frame. Schoolbags of a sort were obligatory, and Woolworths store in Edinburgh had a special line in these at sixpence each. They were made of a sort of stiffened cotton and bound at the seams with a black stuff. Once the fabric got wet they lost all shape and little round black flecks came off the binding and stuck to what at first was our solitary schoolbook. This was a first reader with the unlikely title of *Chick Locken Goes to School*. We had to cover this at home with brown paper but mother, ever artistic, showed me how to use a scrap of wallpaper to make a gay and neat cover, of which I was inordinately proud.

CHAPTER
SEVEN

Learning English

The determining difference between the farm children and the village children was that the farm children arrived at school and immediately they were expected to learn in a language, the English language, which was completely and utterly foreign to them.

The village children of course spoke Scots, or at least they did so outside the school and for the most part in the home as well. Those whose parents aspired to better things were discouraged from speaking Scots in the home and were forced to speak what their parents imagined to be English. In our particular case, my father spoke English with an Irish accent and idiom and my mother spoke the English of the Scots middle classes, but outside the home and school we spoke Scots, and would have been regarded as curiosities if we hadn't done so. Our Scots, the village Scots, was interlarded with secondhand Americanisms like "swell" and "OK" which we regarded as the height of fashion. We tended not to use the archaic and lovely Scots words for which there is no English equivalent and which makes the Scots language so exact and expressive. Our Scots was dismissed as "slang" by people like mother, and we were constantly reprimanded for using it.

For the farm children there was no other language but Scots; they spoke Scots in the home and it was the first and, until they went to school, usually the only language they had ever heard. It is important to remember that these Scots speakers didn't just use different words from the English, but they spoke and thought in an entirely different idiom. To them it was difficult to express themselves in understandable English in even its most basic form.

At five years of age these little, cold and poorly clad and fed children would be herded into a classroom and immediately bawled at by some spinster, herself trying to claw her way out of the working class, in a language which was as foreign to them as French or Italian. It was common for some poor child to look around the classroom in bewilderment and, if he was lucky, some helpful and bilingual classmate would whisper a translation before he or she was faced with the feared "tawse". "She wants tae ken whit name yer ca'ed," the translator would mutter, and relief would spread across the simple face of the questioned infant.

Then came the problem of a reply, and in many cases it would be a problem which remained with the farm child until he was eventually released from the purgatory of school or had slowly sunk to the dunces' section where he could, if lucky, spend the rest of his days in bored oblivion.

Anyone who speaks a foreign language imperfectly will know the process of mental translation which has to be undergone continually during the course of conversation with a native. This was mainly the lot of farm children throughout their school lives. Thus they were condemned as slow, or "donert" as they themselves would express it. Of course any of them bold enough to reply in Scots to a question in English was immediately reprimanded, if not physically punished with the "tawse". The teacher knew the Scots language perfectly well and had at one time spoken it herself. Occasionally it was pressed into service, such as the odd poem read aloud on the birthday of Robert Burns as a reluctant but obligatory duty, but as a language Scots was despised as being the tongue of the poor and the ignorant, and anyone who chose to speak it was considered at best slightly comical but more usually a boor and an oaf. A very few and mainly ancient people in and around the village who spoke Scots and no English at all received the kind of confused admiration that the Victorian English reserved for their faithful Highland servants or the untamed tribesmen of the North-West Frontier but, in the main, the aim of our schooling was to turn us into anglicised Scots.

We would of course never be real English; that was accepted and understood. We were, however, taught in English, and taught moreover to despise our own tongue. Later on, as we "progressed" into higher school, we were taught the history of England, with Bannockburn thrown in. We were given English poetry and literature to read and, with luck and if we were bright enough, we could finish up like our schoolteachers, conscious of having achieved a good third-rate education and without any sense of identity and national pride.

This picture is a bleak one, and as I grew older I found that there were many fine teachers who disagreed with the system although none dared to do so openly, simply because it was the system, and to a large extent, shorn of its more vicious aspects, it remains the system today, not merely at infant school but right through to university. As a result your typical lowland Scot is inarticulate, with all the inherent aggression of those who find difficulty in expressing themselves.

Discipline was kept at our school by the very simple expedient of the free and ready use of the "tawse" right from the infant class and on. The tawse is that most Scottish kind of strap which consists of a leather thong cut into strips at its business end. Each teacher by tradition bought his or her own tawse, and for specially heinous offences a more severe belting was administered by the headmistress. There were many tales of the special qualities of the various tawses kept by different teachers, and in later life we would retail legends of how particularly dreaded instruments were actually fried in such concoctions as salty water.

Our first teacher was known as Miss Stott, and for some mysterious reason she had the reputation of being a good and understanding teacher amongst the parents of the village. Miss Stott was an ancient, near

49

to retirement, but she used her tawse with enthusiasm, mostly of course on the unfortunate farm children. Two of these started their scholastic careers with me, and I was able to chart their progress as they moved yearly into higher classes having exhausted the possibilities of each teacher's tawse and the permutations of punishment it could inflict. Of course I believe that there were even at this early date at least theoretical restrictions which limited the use of the tawse. It was not supposed to be used for intellectual inability but for disobedience, and it was only supposed to be given on the palm of the hand. Both of these restrictions were freely ignored, but nonetheless a teacher had to exercise discretion. It was a stupid teacher for instance who would belt a child whose parents had some sort of standing in the village, such as the children of the local chemist and, if the tawse had to be used on pupils such as these, it was only under the strictest circumstances.

For most children, however, who were often knocked about at home anyway, the teacher knew that they would keep their mouths shut as in all possibility a complaint at home would only lead to a further hammering and, even if a parent disapproved, it would be few who would walk three miles or more to school to make the point, and still less who would be listened to.

So it was that my two classmates, James Honeysett and the appropriately named Alfie Aitken, were belted almost daily and often several times a day during their years at school. Both boys were good-natured and both at an early age gave up any attempt to learn more than was absolutely necessary to be noticed as little as possible. Perhaps because of their very qualities, they were passed along from class to class as good-natured butts of their teachers' verbal scorn and physical abuse. We were always invited to laugh at the witticisms directed too easily at these boys, and this we did with the sense of mingled shame and relief that it was not being done to us, that I am sure has been experienced by other children in other lands who have baited little Jews or negroes.

James Honeysett could make flutes from willow sticks. This he did by carefully working the bark loose and slipping it off in one piece. He then cut the willow with a special skill I could never master and slipped the bark back on again. He never showed or played these lovely instruments at school. I am sure it would have caused universal embarrassment, and he was too kind a person for that. He could trap rabbits and he showed me at least this skill, and he could catch little trout with a "girn", his own fine snare.

I admired James Honeysett and would walk miles to the farm where he lived, taking the shortcut along the railway line. When the nights were short, we would go to the bothy on the farm. This was where the single workers lived and where they sat round the fire in the evenings and talked. I could walk home along the line, counting out the sleepers and knowing that the glow from the sunset lay to the west, which was where the village was. James Honeysett taught me more than the school ever taught him. He was killed in the war, I think.

CHAPTER
EIGHT

School and Singing

My sisters had previously been taught in the infants'
class by Miss Stott and she knew us as a studious
family who actually liked school. Nonetheless it was
not long before I got my first taste of the tawse from
her. I needed to pee and I did not know what to do
about it. The procedure of raising the hand and asking
for permission to go to the toilet had never been
explained to me. "Please miss, a want tae pee," said
one new recruit on his first day and was promptly told
to ask properly; not knowing how, he was silently
wetting his trousers. I needed to as well and didn't
know what to do either. I whispered my predicament
to the little girl sitting next to me and to demonstrate
my urgent need I put her hand on the top of my
trousers, where I was already starting to leak. Miss
Stott had a dirty mind, and sex to her, or fancied sex,
had to be strangled at birth. She called me out and
gave me a taste of the tawse without, as I thought, any
reason and thus with a sense of injustice which has
remained with me to this day.

Another time we were asked to draw a picture of a
ship on our slates. Drawing was something of which I

was particularly fond, and in no time I had drawn what I thought was a very good fishing boat. Since I had both time and a space on my slate, I drew in the bottom of the sea as well with a big crab walking along the shore. Miss Stott, sadly, had no sense of humour and imagined my mind was a much more devious instrument than that of the normal five-year-old. She took it, in other words, that I was trying to make a fool of her, and for this fancied slight I again tasted the tawse.

I didn't spend long at the old school, for it was only a few months after father died that we finally moved into the new building. This marked a tremendous change for the better, both in that the new school was only a very short distance from our house and that it had previously undreamed-of luxuries such as central heating, cloakrooms where the pipes dried out the sodden garments of those children who had walked in the rain from the farms, and a gymnasium where we all congregated in the morning to sing a hymn and be told how lucky we were to live in Britain and not one of the far-off heathen lands dominated by want, fear and ignorance. "From Greenland's icy mountains", we chanted, "to India's coral strands . . . they call us to deliver their land from error's chains", and if we thought at all about the words, we saw nothing incongruous there.

We also sang the national anthem, and here the big boys at the back of the assembly who commonly kept their mouths shut or, to escape later belting, moved them soundlessly, would join in with unexpected zest.

53

"May he protect our laws and ever give us cause" we innocents would sing, while behind us the big boys, or at least the bolder of them, would sing, "May he protect our laws and never scratch his ba's". "Stay behind, the boys in that row," Mrs McKenzie would announce at the end of assembly. "It wisnae me, Miss," each one would protest, and the innocent were punished too, so that the guilty could not escape.

Singing, or at least what passed for singing, was important in our early schooling, for we were taught our tables by a system of chanting. "One and one is two, two and two are four, three and three are six," we would chant in unison, and passers-by outside the school window would stop and listen.

The McVeighs in any case were all good singers. Father sang all the Irish songs he knew and those music-hall numbers with an Irish flavour such as "Paddy you're a villain, Paddy you're a rogue, there's nothing of you Irish except your name and brogue. You're killing me by inches, I know I am your slave. But when you're dead, upon my soul, I'll dance upon your grave".

Mother had a sweet singing voice. Before she was married she had gone round hospitals singing hymns on Sundays, and she especially enjoyed the Moody and Sankey belters like "The old rugged cross". She loved the old ballads as well, and her favourite of all songs was that most powerful of old Scots ballads "The bonny Earl o' Moray". It was a long time after father's death before she sang again, but when she did and when she sang the "Earl o' Moray" we fell silent and listened captivated as she also was, both by her own singing and by the wonderful old Scots words: "Ye hielan's and ye lawlan's" she would start, and we settled down to listen as people have done for centuries, enthralled by the music and the tale. "They have slain the Earl o' Moray and laid him on the green." A tear would start in mother's eye at the beauty of the song and the intensity of her own feeling, and suddenly the despised old Scots tongue would have dignity and meaning: "He was a braw callant and he red at the ring, O the bonnie Earl o' Moray, he micht hae been a king. Ah, lang shall the leddies look frae the castle doon, ere they see the Earl o' Moray gae soondin thru' the toon," she would finish and we were silent for a little and we felt proud of our mother.

Negro Spirituals, no doubt politically unacceptable nowadays, we all loved to sing. Mother would commence, "Swing low sweet chariot, coming for to carry me home." Then we would join in, "Swing low sweet chariot, coming for to carry me home." "I looked over Jordan and what did I see?" Mother would sing and we would respond. "A Band of angels, comin' after me, comin' to carry me home."

Moving on from the sacred to the secular, Mother would render one of her own favourites. "Just a song at twilight, when the lights are low. And the flickering shadows, softly come and go. Though the way be weary and the road be long. Still to us at twilight, comes love's own song. Comes love's own sweet song." I fancy mother thought of our father and of their own love when she sang these words.

Although we were always rebuked for speaking "slang" at home, Mother had a rich store of Scots ballads. These were the kind of songs which once every bothy lad knew by heart and indeed were still a familiar feature of our own musical landscape. "Auld Robin Gray" told the story of a young girl in love and her tragic loss. "Young Jamie loo'ed me weel and socht me for his bride. But saving a croon, he had naething else beside. Tae mak the croon a poond, young Jamie went tae sea. And auld Robin Gray, cam a coortin me." But Jamie was drowned at sea. "The boat it was awrack and for tears I could nae see. But auld Robin Gray, he is guid tae me." All these old ballads had a story to tell although perhaps, to modern ears, they might seem somewhat maudlin.

"The Crooked Bawbee" was best sung as a duet. A young beggar lass was given a crooked old bawbee as the only coin a herd boy, almost as poor, has. The years pass and the lad prospers and becomes the Laird of Glenshee but the girl is as poor as ever. They have never forgotten each other and they meet once more. He tells her she can have every kind of riches if only she will marry him and go off to Glenshee, but she is ever faithful to her first love. "Ye can claithe me in satin and mak me a lady, but I'll no gae wi' ye tae bonny Glenshee. For the heart that beats under this auld ragged plaidie, Is true tae the lad o' the crooked bawbee." Then the Laird reveals who he is. "Sae ye are the laddie wha gied me the penny. The lad that I'll loo to the day that I dee. Ye can claithe me in satin and mak me a lady and I will gae wi' ye tae bonny Glenshee."

56

Norah had a lovely singing voice which was to develop into a contralto that could have led to a training and a stage career if we had had the money or had lived in another country. Mollie sang too, and Kathleen copied all the latest romantic hits on the radio, then just starting to make its appearance among the more affluent in the village. Marion delighted in comic songs picked up from the most unlikely sources, such as one in praise of whisky sung by the church beadle when he was drunk, and therefore sung frequently. "Twelve and a tanner a bottle," Marion would sing with complete staggering effects, "Look whit it's costin' the day, twelve and a tanner the bottle, it taks a' the pleesure away. An' afore ye can get a wee drappie, ye hae tae spend a' that ye've goat. Hoo can a fella be happy, when happiness coasts sic' a loat?" There were but two songs in the beadle's repertoire. He sang about the price of whisky when drunk but when sober, or on the way to being drunk, he had a rousing patriotic number which we all knew by heart, called "Pin your faith to the motherland".

Pin your faith to the motherland, the dearest land
  on earth,
Pin your faith to the motherland, the land that
  gave you birth,
Englishmen and Irishmen, Scotsmen and Welshmen
  too-oo-oo-oo.
Pin your faith to the motherland, and she'll pin
  hers to you.

As for me, blessed or cursed with a retentive memory, I picked up almost every tune and song I heard and sang them with enthusiasm and an utter lack of discrimination, unless it was a preference for anything which seemed to have an Irish flavour. The largely secret and vital tradition of Irish ballad music which was so much alive in the bothies of the farms, particularly during the seasonal visits of the Irish labourers, was to remain unknown to me for a few years, and is a later part of this story.

There were no male teachers in our school. There had been a headmaster, but he was killed under most singular circumstances just about the time of father's death. He was also boy-scout master for the village troop and, ex-soldier that he was, he was keen on teaching the older boys how to shoot. This he did on a small range with light .22 rifles and, during the course of this instruction, one of the boys accidentally shot him in the head, killing him instantly. His widow had been a schoolteacher and she was straight away elevated to her dead husband's post.

Mrs McKenzie was a large lady and no doubt quite kindly as a person. She taught the senior class at school as well as being headmistress, and thus I seldom made her acquaintance except for one or two occasions when my temper got the better of me. This would usually be at some outrage committed by a bully, of whom there was always a goodly supply. These battles commenced in the playground, and no matter what the size or strength of the aggressor, I would lay into him if my temper was roused. At those times I was carried, kicking and shouting threats, bodily to the headmistress by the school janitor (the one who had done my father out of a job) and, trembling with rage, I would submit to Mrs McKenzie's tawse, heeding little and caring less.

I once found a purse in the village street. It had keys and money inside, six or seven pound notes, which was more money than I had ever even thought of. An enclosure showed that it belonged to our headmistress and I took it right away to her house. I was about seven at the time and I did not feel any particular virtue in the act. Both father and mother had taught us honesty and they were utterly honest themselves. It would just never have occurred to any of us to keep any money we found. I rang the bell and explained to the maid who answered the door that I had found the headmistress's purse, which I handed to her. The maid asked me to wait and I did so at the doorstep. Shortly she came back and handed me two pennies and closed the door.

CHAPTER
NINE

The New School;
Village Entertainment

As I have said, the new school was a great improvement, and somehow this seemed, to an extent at least, to rub off on both pupils and staff. The children still walked to school, of course. The farthest farm in the parish was almost four miles away, and although Haddington was much nearer to it, the children from this farm had to walk to our school, in snow, rain, and along the dark unlit roads of winter.

I don't know if it was merely a process of gradual improvement or if it was the result of political change, but just about that time even the conditions of the farm workers took a turn for the better. Agriculture was in the grip of the general depression which had taken hold of the country. The richest arable land in Scotland was to a large extent reverting to pasture. One cannot blame the farmer too much who depressed his workers' wages because the country was being flooded with Danish and Irish bacon and cheap American and Canadian wheat but, as always, the poor suffered most, simply because their margin between poverty and destitution was so narrow.

Nonetheless government grants came out which provided the means to give sanitation and running water to cottages that had previously lacked both of these things. I have travelled over the same roads today and I see hardly any arable land in East Lothian which is not given over to the ubiquitous potato followed by a crop, often three crops, of barley. I can still trace the wells with their rusty standpipes, often blocked by mud and leaves now, which were the sole source of water for each group of cottages. The little kitchens and water closets, built to a standard pattern of brick in the early 1930s, still for the most part are there, tacked on to the stone cottage rows, but the heaps of excrement waiting to be carted out to the fields have long since vanished.

Wages remained depressed; a ploughman or an orraman would "fee" for sixty or seventy pounds a year with his cottage and some potatoes supplied and his wife or children working "at the piece", hoeing or singling turnips or stacking at threshing time. In those days large gangs of women at these tasks were a feature of lowland Scotland. There might be as many as fifteen women and girls hoeing up the rows in the great fields which still form so much of the Lothian landscape. Each one wore a home-made sunbonnet of linen or cotton stitched onto a wire frame and protecting both the head and the back of the neck. I believe these bonnets were called "uglys", or so at least I have seen them listed in present-day museum exhibits, but to us they were "grevits", which would appear to be a corruption of "cravat".

With the new school, we now aspired to higher and cleaner things. There was hot malted milk at tuppence a week for those who could afford it, although jam and bread "pieces" still formed the lunch of the farm children. Slates were abolished for all but the infant classes, and a gym mistress and even a cookery class staffed by itinerant teachers made their appearance. My sisters came home with an assortment of buns and sausage rolls for which they had to pay and these, no matter how badly baked, were of course eagerly eaten.

Dances and like functions were now held in the new school hall, and at these mother always made up a part of the catering staff. For this work she was paid a small wage and her "pauckle", the Scots word for the English "perk", consisting in this case of remainders of trifle and the kind of sandwiches which had egg and cress in them with the crusts cut off and curly ends. For years I was convinced that this was the way that the rich lived, on a diet of trifle and curly sandwiches, and I resolved that one day we should all eat this fare as a matter of course. Meanwhile mother, when we were specially hard-up, would send me with a little note to the grocer. When mother sent me with a note this meant that she had no money at all and the grocer or the chemist or even, on odd occasions, the chip shop, had a polite and beautifully written request for a few coppers' credit. This was seldom refused, for mother always paid her debts. Long after we had left the village, mother would send me in the bus with a few shillings against her outstanding debt to the grocer, until it was finally paid. When we had nothing else to eat, mother's note would be a request for a half loaf of bread "sliced with the hammy knife". This was the grocer's slicing machine on which the ham and bacon were cut, and if he sliced the loaf through the machine it imparted the flavour of the ham, if not the substance.

The new school had annual prize days when, spruced up, there we would sit with those parents who chose to attend, and the lucky or cleverer pupils would get copies of *Black Beauty* or *Treasure Island*. Inevitably the McVeighs would take the lion's share of these and, since we were a family of voracious readers and because the village was without a public library, they were passed on and backwards, exchanged and quarreled over, becoming both dog-eared and so well read that we knew them almost by heart, and indeed on wet Sundays we acted them out as plays.

There was always a concert of sorts at these annual prizegivings; something we called a "cantata", which I suppose was a sort of musical play. One year the girls acted out something called "Pandora's Box". This was a surprise number where the box, a muslin-covered tea chest, was placed over a trapdoor on the stage. The open end of the box was over the trapdoor and the top had been sawn by the janitor to form a lid. Pandora tapped on the lid and, at rehearsals, the little girls clad as home-made fairies had been trained to emerge through the box from their waiting position underneath the stage. At the actual performance, when Pandora at first gaily and then with increasing panic tapped and later hammered on the lid, nothing happened, for one of the big boys had nailed the lid firmly shut. By the usual process of collective threats, this time left to the janitor, and to cries of "It wisnae me," the incorrigible Alfie Aitken was established as the culprit. Alfie took his hammering with a quiet grin and his usual good nature. He was leaving school in any event, and a hammering was the price he expected to pay.

In those days, when there was no television, when even the wireless was a novelty and when few people had the money, in any event, to travel and go to the cinema or theatre at Edinburgh, the village had a steady stream of concerts and similar events. By dint of dogged rehearsals, fluctuating cast lists, bickering and worries, these events were finally staged to a more or less captive audience, for families and extended families, cousins, uncles and aunts and in-laws — "guid brothers and guid sisters" — were both more numerous and much closer then. The boy scouts, the church organ fund or even the long-suffering African mission would therefore benefit by ten pounds or so. Tickets would be sold by suitable conscripts, who were instructed in the right technique of "chapping" on doors: "Dinnae gang tae the big hoose, ye're wastin' yer time. Hoo the hell dae ye think they got there in the first place if it wisnae by bein' mean? Sell yer tickets on a Friday nicht when they've been paid, and wait till they've had their tea."

By the middle of the 1930s there was also a jazz band in the village. This consisted of trumpet, saxophone, drums and clarinet. The radio and the second-hand "American" ideas it disseminated were beginning to influence what, for want of a better term, might be described as our village cultural life. Such expensive musical instruments as those required by a jazz band were of course out of the question for working-class youth, but the band was formed from the middle-class residents in the village. A captive audience was required on which they could exercise their new but dubious talents and so, until they could move into the exalted spheres dominated by Henry Hall and Harry Roy, the village proved to be a convenient testing ground.

The leader of the band, who inevitably was the saxophonist, was the son of a large house in the village sustained by a fashionable and expensive hairdressing establishment in Edinburgh. His enterprise was assisted by another young man, who played the drums and came from an even better-heeled background than the hairdresser's son. He was a powerful but tiny man, afflicted with some kind of dwarfism. His name was Uppman, and inevitably he was always known as "wee Uppman". He drove around in a yellow sports car and he was liked and admired for his pluck. When I was about nine years old he went to bed one night and shot himself through the head with a revolver that his father had brought home from the war.

Since the band was a four-piece outfit, it was difficult for one of the musicians to stop playing and to double up as a vocalist. This was the time when every band had to have a vocalist who could sing songs like "I met her on the beach at Bali Bali" or "Tiptoe through the tulips", or cowboy numbers like "We are wanderers of the waste-land". A promising youth called Jim Mall, who was by profession an unemployed painter, was co-opted as vocalist and we all thought that he was a borderline genius who must inevitably graduate to the big time. Jim Mall would come on the stage only after the band had completed the first few bars and would go up to the microphone, an instrument which we had previously neither heard of nor seen. He wore a sharp suit with wide bell-bottom trousers and a short jacket in the high fashion known as a "bum-freezer" and he had a fag in his mouth. Jim was no great shakes as a singer, but he had stage presence. He also had a Clark Gable moustache and long sideburns. Taking his Woodbine out of his mouth, he would stick one cheek up against the microphone and sing: "We are wanderers of the waste-land, ma lob-eyed mule, ma broken-down horse and me. Always travellin' on the waste-land, ma lop-eared mule, ma broken-down horse and me." Or: "When a wis young, a used tae be a rip-a-roarin' son of a gun in ol' Wyomin'. A loved a girl, she took ma pal, so a saddled ma horse and bridled ma mule and then a took tae rovin'." Having finished his song, sung in accents which both we and he imagined to be American but were mainly broad East Lothian Scots, Jim would replace the Woodbine in his mouth, turn on his heel without the slightest acknowledgement of the plaudits of his audience, and walk off the stage. Jim Mall may have been a bit short on talent but he had, as I say, presence. He became an air-gunner during the war.

The "Soirée" was much more informal and it required little rehearsal, for the performers were all regulars who could be called on to give their known "piece". Here the funds were usually raised by a collection; the notice always bore the intimidatory announcement "Silver Collection", which meant that we had to contribute at least a thruppenny bit.

There was one lady in the village who was so dedicated to staging cantatas that it amounted almost to a vice. This was a spinster schoolteacher who lived with her mother and who taught in a school at nearby Prestonpans. We laughed at poor Miss Beattie and told the most outrageous tales about her behind her back. She had a passion for things Japanese, her house was festooned with bamboo and she wore a kimono in the evenings. So many of these women schoolteachers were fated to remain unmarried. They had grimly levered themselves a little out of their own class, and thus few would ever marry a carpenter or a mechanic. At the same time, few men from a better-off background would be interested in them. As civil servants, once they married they lost their permanent status and became either unemployed or mere "temporaries" liable to dismissal and without pension rights. Many of them, too, had aged parents to support, parents who had often made the great sacrifices necessary to let their children "get on". All we saw of course was the sarcastic and sometimes comical side to those people but, as children, we did not understand the sadness so often behind the situation.

Thus Miss Beattie continued to stage her cantatas and recruit the village children. Most of them would turn up at rehearsal night solely to make fun of her or play tricks. The inevitable Alfie Aitken, who had got a job in the village, came along smoking his first Woodbines and giving small boys a "draw", so that half the potential cast lay sick on the church green. After a week or two, most of the children got bored and the serious casting could begin. The McVeighs, who were always great joiners, remained amongst this hard core, as did a large family of a couple who both, father and mother, fancied them as musically talented.

We staged one cantata which employed a sort of action round a song going: "There was a tree, a very fine tree, and on this tree there was a branch, and on this branch there was a twig, and on this twig there was a nest, and in this nest there was an egg", etcetera, etcetera. As each line unfolded, an extra singer would come on stage carrying the branch, the nest, and so on. The youngest member of the musical family, a lad of about my own age which would be seven or so, had been given the part of coming on stage with a giant egg to end the song. This he did but, with a good case of stage fright at his first big part, he proceeded to pee his trousers as the whole company sang: "And the green grass grew around around, and the green grass grew around." I watched with satisfaction, for I did not like that boy, and the audience were enthralled.

The next cantata was an ambitious musical about castaways on a desert island. There were wrecked seamen and fairies who came to the rescue and comic

natives of the "coon" blackface variety, who sang
and told each other riddles and limericks. The natives
had to be dressed in pyjamas, and here Miss Beattie
had her first problem, for most of us slept in our shirts.
The pyjamas, obtained from various and presumably
middle-class sources, were eventually distributed in
sufficient quantity to include even me in the company.
I may explain here that, since mother was often at
work, I had to go where my sisters went. In this way I
went to the Brownies regularly enough to be accepted
more or less as a sort of male supercargo. Since the
McVeigh sisters had some known vocal and histrionic
talents, and since they had been trained by their
parents to take the obligations of life seriously, they
were always in demand for village concerts. Patrick
therefore had to be fitted in somehow as part of the
agreed price, and in this case I was one of the natives.
"Who are the lightest men in the world, Rastus?" my
feed had to ask me, and I would reply, "Why, the men
of Ayr to be sure." "No, Rastus," the feed had to cap,
"I think it must be the men of Cork."

As can readily be seen, the subtlety of wit in such
productions was not of a very high order. Norah, I
think, was one of the castaways and Mollie was the
good fairy "Wish to Learn". Marion was the fairy
"Sleepyhead", a much more fetching character: "Oh I
am fairy Sleepyhead, I never can get up from bed. I've
wakened from a lovely dream, of sliding down a fine
sunbeam." Norah sang a song about a dead bird:
"Poor little skylark, sweet little bird. Your song in the

69

meadow oft I have heard. Now sunk in silence, no saviour nigh, within your gilded cage at last you'll pine and droop and die."

This was all heady and unfamiliar culture to both audience and players. Outside in the streets, the same little girls would play skipping and sing: "Katie Bairdie haud a coo, black an' white aboot the coo; wisnae that a bonny wee coo, daunce Katie Bairdie." The idea of composing, far less of performing, a cantata based on these old Scots play songs would of course have been treated with amused derision. Yet we had a rich store of street ballads, some of which had come down to us sifted through the Victorian music halls, but many of which were truly of the streets and anonymous village wit, and all of which we knew by heart.

"Oor Jock's a sodger," we would bawl, running along the street or swinging off a rope tied to the branch of a tree, "He comes frae Aebyhill; he gets his pay on a Setterday and then he buys hauf a gill. He gauns tae the kirk on Sunday, hauf an oor late, He pu's the buttons off his shirt and pits them on the plate." We even dispensed medical advice: "Paraffin ile, paraffin ile. Drink it like beer when ye're bad wi' the bile. Drink it like beer and lie doon on the flair An' ye'll never be bothered wi' the bile ony mair."

We sang in the streets, of course, and no one thought us strange. In the school we were taught: "When the leaves bedeck the trees with green, lovely green, verdant green." As usual, the big boys remained silent or mouthed the words, but irrepressible souls like Alfie Aitken would bawl: "When the leaves bedeck the trees

70

with grease, lovely grease, verdigris." Life to Alfie was one big hammering, but he considered it well worthwhile. Left to ourselves in our children's world, we knew dozens of the auld sangs, and the airs to many more. Every boy could whistle and many more could play the mouth-organ. A shilling Hohner was our great ambition to own, but many boys learned to play by a sort of primitive hire system whereby a mouth-organ could be leased for the length of time it took to read a comic paper. Risks of infection from the mingled saliva were taken care of by each player giving the instrument a vigorous rub on the sleeve of his jersey.

One of our next-door neighbours had a son who was fanatically attached to his "moothie". Jock Mackay was, in fact, a bit simple but he played the mouth organ with the most tremendous enthusiasm. His repertoire consisted solely of Scots tunes and mainly bagpipe airs at that, and for this accomplishment he was not without fame in the village. Looking back now, I realise that Jock's musical gifts were but slight. He was no Larry Adler but, as so often happens with a simple child, his mother was over-protective towards him and tended to fight his battles, often moreover seeing a slight where none was intended.

On one such occasion I had fallen out with Jock and he had complained to his mother, who had at once addressed her son's grievances to mine. This she detailed in loud tones over the garden fence and then, suddenly remembering that the previous day, when in good humour, she had presented my mother with a plate of home-baked scones, she shouted: "An' ye can gies back the scones I gie'd ye."

CHAPTER TEN

The Chip Shops

Life without laughter, especially to us children, was inconceivable. As always, however, tragedy and laughter steered a course which came close to being one.

There was a travelling chip shop in the village, owned by a Mr Young. If Jock Haborn had by general consent been voted the village drunk, Mr Young must have come a close second. As the owner of a small business, he faced the inevitable hazard of those who deal in cash, which is the feeling of affluence when there are a few bob in the till. Mr Young would start out on his rounds, the horse fed and watered, the fire stoked and the potatoes all peeled and cut to size, lying in buckets of water to prevent them turning brown. This preparatory work had been undertaken by Mr Young's wife and his three daughters, ever hopeful that the chip business would boom and flourish.

Full of optimism, with the chimney belching black smoke, chip shop, Mr Young and the horse (who knew the way) would start off on the round. Sadly, after the first few shillings had been gathered in, Mr Young would turn the horse around and head for the village grocer. His intentions no doubt were of the best, and he only needed a couple of bottles of beer to cope with a sudden onset of thirst. Within an hour or two, the beer had become whisky and the travelling chip shop had degenerated into a shambles of greasy, half-cooked chips, with a fire which eventually guttered and died.

It was then that Mr Young felt first guilt and then remorse, which was quickly followed by rage that his wife and daughters had let him down so scandalously in their haphazard preparations for the chipper's evening round. He would poke his head through the front hatch, grasp the reins and give them a jerk, muttering to the horse, who knew all too well what was coming: "Come oan, ye bugger," and he would head for home. One evening, word having quickly gone round the village that Mr Young was "fleein'", his wife and daughters, knowing what was coming to them, fled the house and took refuge with us. Mother bundled them upstairs and we all prepared for the inevitable siege, which came within half an hour or so.

In answer to Mr Young's thunderous knocking on our door, mother shouted to him to go home and be properly ashamed of himself in the morning, which of course she knew he would be. Mr Young's dander, however, was well and truly up. Unable to get into the house by the door and seeing his wife and daughters at the upstairs window, he grabbed a ladder lying at the side of the wall and started to climb up. Mother immediately opened the door and, holding the ladder by its foot, she started to shake it with all her might: "Get down from that ladder at once," she commanded. "You ought to be ashamed of yourself, James Young. Get down or I'll shake you down, and get down on your knees and pray to God for forgiveness." I have never known my gentle mother to be in such a fury of rage and indignation, ever since that day. First out of terror, Mr Young slid down the ladder and then, out of sudden shame and remorse, he did kneel down and actually pray with mother that God would forgive him.

It would be pleasant to record that Mr Young became a reformed character, but life is like that only in the Victorian temperance novels that we used to get for nothing from the detritus of village jumble sales. Mr Young did stay off the booze for a bit, but he soon went back on the batter. Then the horse and the chipper had to be sold and tragedy struck yet again, for Mrs Young was taken off to the hospital with advanced tuberculosis of the lungs.

Tuberculosis, which we always called "consumption", was a familiar yet dreaded scourge to us. Almost all families had at least one member or a close relative who had been tapped on the shoulder by that dreadful ghost and spirited off to hospital, usually never to return. The Youngs' eldest daughter tried against all the odds to keep both drunken father and the rest of the family together while her mother lay dying, but it was a battle this brave and intelligent girl of twelve years or so was doomed to lose. Soon the family was broken up, the children dispersed to relatives and charitable homes, and Mr Young to God knows where.

The village, however, was not to remain chipless for long, for soon a new chip shop was started by an entrepreneur of a very different sort. Matt Hardie was the village part-time postman. He was a widower and he had been a machine-gunner during the war, having like father been severely wounded but without the social advantage of a lost limb. Matt built a chip shop in his back garden out of odd wood and corrugated iron. This of course was before the days of such bureaucratic inventions as planning permission. Once the chip shop was completed and its copper range installed, Matt painted it a deep maroon red both inside and out.

The reason for Matt's colour scheme was that he supported the famous and beloved Edinburgh football team, Heart of Midlothian, and this was their colour. To say that Matt supported the Hearts was of course an understatement, for he gave to this team, win or lose, the same devotion as Saint Francis gave to God.

When I grew older, I took it as no coincidence that the colours of the post office were maroon and black. If they had been anything else, Matt would have resigned or repainted his bicycle and hat band. As it was, his house and his fence and his chip shop were all painted maroon and Matt himself, summer and winter, wore a maroon jersey. He was a small man and he had both a kind nature and a kind face, despite a bad scar from the war. He managed the village football team with some of the surplus enthusiasm he had from the support of his idols, and for some baffling reason this team was called the "Longniddry Bluebells". They nevertheless wore maroon jerseys which Matt himself washed, and it was a brave sight in the evening to see the eleven maroon jerseys on the front green at the side of the maroon-painted house but in front of the maroon chip shop, whose corrugated iron roof was likewise coloured maroon. If, by some chemistry, the smoke from the chimney could have been dyed maroon, I am sure that Matt would have been a happy man.

As it was, in later years Matt fell in love with mother and, in a quiet way, I am sure she was fond of him. They never married, although he would come up to see her when we moved into Edinburgh, and during the war when I was serving abroad, mother wrote to say that their friendship had ended. I thought it very sad for them both, but I knew that for mother the only man she would ever love lay long dead with nothing to mark his grave but that little glass dome with the artificial flowers and the tablet with his name on it.

"Hurrah for the Longniddry Bluebells," we used to sing, "Longniddry's fitba' team. And if by chance they win the cup, hoo Hardie's face will beam." About the same time as the village got its new school, politics decreed that it was also to be supplied with a proper playing field. The layout of a proper football pitch was, I suppose, both right and necessary, although it destroyed the mushroom beds which were a source of some slight income to me. In a village with woods and trees and streams galore, and with the seashore with its endless fascinations only a few yards away, it was the height of bureaucratic ignorance to provide a roundabout, swings and a swing-boat for children who could make their own amusements. For the first few weeks we sampled these "amusements" and then we went back to playing Tarzan in the woods, to catching minnows and eels in the burns and to exploring the rock pools down by the sea. The swings and the swing-boat were deserted except for the big boys who went there to smoke their Woodbines, cough and chat up the not so big girls, who would sneak off down to the playing field wearing their big sisters' stockings and with a hasty smear of lipstick applied by touch after they had left the house.

Longniddry was a railway junction on a small scale, and about ten railwaymen and their families lived there. These had limited free travel by rail, of course, and just prior to one Christmas two of the railway wives went up to Edinburgh to do their Christmas shopping. Probably because it was a cold day, or even because they felt like it, they partook of a little refreshment in the buffet before returning and by the time they got back to the village they were really "fleein'".

Once off the train, they headed down to the playing field and, one on either end of the swing-boat, they proceeded to "beam" it back and forward, at the same time bursting into song. It was not long before a goodly part of the village had assembled to watch, and before long the two husbands themselves were summoned from work. A swing-boat is a heavy thing and dangerous to try to stop once it is in determined motion. The husbands therefore had to wait until the fun was exhausted, and meanwhile the wives were bawling the ditty: "Old King Cole was a merry old soul, and a merry old soul was he. He sat on a rock and played with his cock and he rattled his ba's in the sea."

CHAPTER
ELEVEN

Port Seton and the Plymouth Brethren

Apart from the railwaymen and the increasing middle-class community who used the place as a dormitory, Longniddry served an agricultural community. Just along the coast, however, about three miles away, was another village, Port Seton, which revolved almost entirely around its harbour and fishing fleet. From the age of seven or so, this place fascinated me and I would walk there frequently just to look at the boats and to talk to the fisher folk. It was remarkable how close-knit and self-contained a community this was. Most of the boats were small, from about five to twenty tons. For the most part the days of sail were gone, but many boats had both an engine and a lug sail which helped them stay close to the wind. Some had a little deckhouse but many had only a cockpit, and they all smelt abominably of fish and stale diesel oil. Still, I longed for the day when I could leave school and go to sea, an ambition I never realised.

The boats all had beautiful names; the *Budding Rose*, *Protect Me*, *Bountiful Harvest*, *Dunottar Castle*, *Mary*

Love and the *Good Shepherd*. Along the harbour wall the retired fishermen would sit mending the nets, and some would knit jerseys of blue oiled wool with four needles in the rapid Shetland fashion. All the fishermen wore jerseys in those days and they were always of a blue wool which was almost black. The jerseys had high collars which buttoned along one shoulder, for it was dangerous when handling nets at sea to have any buttons on the front of the clothing. For the same reason, the fishermen wore brown smocks which had no buttons on them.

On Sundays the fisher folk would wear dark blue trousers and sometimes a jacket over the jersey together with a cloth cap at a nautical angle. Many of the older wives still wore the dark wool overskirt kilted over the blue and white or red and white striped skirt with its petticoats beneath, and on the great festival of the "Fisherman's Walk" all the females, even the little girls, wore this lovely costume.

The Fisherman's Walk was held every autumn at the close of the summer fishing season. Every fishing village held this festival, which indeed still survives to an extent today. Things started in the morning with a procession through the village headed by the local brass or pipe band, and there was dancing in the streets until late at night. At night a huge bonfire was lit with fishboxes piled around an old boat, and this was always the climax to the Walk.

Outsiders were welcome to watch the Walk, but they did not participate in any way. Even the speech of the fisher folk was different from ours. They spoke the purest Scots, but in a very rapid and singsong intonation. So distinctive was this that even in this fishing village, within sight of ours, their speech made them identifiable for what they were.

Some of the fishing community, however, did not participate in the Walk. They did not in fact take any real part in any aspect of the community. These were the members of the sect to which mother's family belonged: the Plymouth Brethren. It seemed to me, and I suppose still does seem, a curious and rather joyless version of Christianity, although mother's religion was compassionate and loving enough. There appeared to be two versions of "the Brethren" as they referred to themselves. Mother's brand was the "Open" or original variety, but there was another branch, presumably of a more zealous mould, the "Closed" Brethren.

It is curious how the human race, particularly in matters of politics or religion, seems to have such an inherent bias towards the creation of schisms. A leader, be it Jan Huss or Karl Marx or Mahomet, proclaims the true faith but soon another leader arises with his own particular version of the truth. So it was with the Close Brethren, who kept themselves to themselves and took no part in the world outside the necessary associations of making a living (at which they were invariably very good). No variety of Brethren read a newspaper except for the weather forecast. No-one listened to the wireless either but in later days, when the fishing boats became bigger and were equipped with short-wave radio, all the Brethren homes had powerful radio sets so that they could keep in touch with their boats at sea and get the weather forecasts and the market prices for fish, and for these uses only.

Needless to say, no-one in the Brethren ever went to the cinema or theatre or a public house and the woman did not wear make-up. This last prohibition did not prevent them dressing, in fact overdressing, expensively with an emphasis on fur coats and dresses which were not considered "suggestive". Mother in fact had little time for much of this nonsense, seeing it for the hypocrisy it was, and when on our trips to Edinburgh we went to the Brethren meeting-house we children, and no doubt mother as well, felt our shabbiness acutely in the presence of so many well-dressed and obviously prosperous adults and children.

We had an "Uncle" who came to live in the village and who had two sisters who lived in the fishing village. These were in fact just distant relatives of mother's. The sisters, both of whom were known as "Pussy", were elderly and mildly insane. They spent their days distributing holy tracts, which they purchased in considerable quantity from their small private income. These they would hide under fish-boxes, convinced that, sometime, an irreligious fisherman would find one, read it and experience the same sort of sudden conversion as St. Paul on the road to Damascus. This after all was the kind of infantile rubbish contained in their tracts; we knew, for they never failed to give them to us or even send them by post. They would make forays into the fields and conduct their crazy missionary work amongst the gangs of women and girls, trying to get them to sing hymns when they stopped at midday to eat their "piece". These women were a tough lot; they had to be, to be fieldworkers, but the "Pussies" persevered and were tolerated with the tolerance that most working-class people have for the do-gooders who never seem to preach to the upper classes.

The brother, "Uncle" Frank Harris, was of an altogether different kind. He had kept a religious bookshop but he was now retired and was a widower. He had one daughter, who was an adopted child and would be about thirty years of age when they came to live in the village. Certainly some of the Brethren, if not all, believed that sexual intercourse outside the need to procreate was sinful, and no doubt today's advances in the techniques of artificial insemination would have pleased them greatly. I have often wondered if Uncle Harris just could not bear to love his wife, even to beget children, but in any event both father and daughter were prigs and busybodies.

As soon as he came to the village, Frank Harris began to interfere in our family life. He had little else to do but ensure that the McVeighs did not continue down their slippery slope to hell along the "worldly" slide of "cantatas", Sunday school and singing secular songs for the sheer hell of it rather than carefully selected hymns which praised God. He would invite us up, usually one by one for we were more vulnerable that way, to his lovely bungalow, for tea. "Remember, we are all born in sin", he would admonish me, at the age of seven. He never had any icing on his cake, as that would be "worldly", and the slices were carefully watched. He would take me for a walk in the garden and question me closely on matters of theology and never offer any of the fruit in which that garden abounded. He never gave me a penny to spend on sweets, which were to course "worldly". Nor did his daughter give us a "hurl" in their motor-car, a treat we all longed for, although she took me to the garage and showed it off with pride.

The daughter, who was misnamed "May", was tall with a large and red nose which dripped. She called her father "Daddy", which struck us as utterly ridiculous, and she sat on his knee and combed his beard, which now I am convinced was kinky.

Frank Harris continually gave mother advice, both religious and secular. The secular advice was largely concerned with the additional economies she could make in the family budget by dispensing with our halfpenny packet of sweets or mother's beloved bar of plain chocolate, a little square of which she always ate at night as her great treat. This advice given, he would proffer half-a-crown to mother, who was expected to be profusely grateful. It could not last that way. One day mother told him to keep both his advice and his money and to go home and ponder what Christianity was all about. Whatever Frank Harris pondered on, it was not the need for humility or forgiveness, for we saw him no more. Not long after mother had given Uncle Frank Harris the bum's rush, we had a knock on our door which mother opened to reveal two strangers, a man and his wife. They must have been in their late thirties although, to me, anyone over twenty or so appeared middle-aged. It transpired that the man, Mr McIntosh, had been a prisoner-of-war with father. Although he lived only a few miles away, near Haddington, he had just heard that father had been living in Longniddry.

The McIntoshes had a smallholding, one of a score or so that the Department of Agriculture had set up for suitable ex-servicemen in East Lothian. Sadly, they did not know of father's death but mother gave them a cup of tea and they had a chat together.

When they were going Mrs McIntosh pressed a ten-shilling note into mother's hand. Mother was reluctant to take the money but Mrs McIntosh replied — and, across all the years, I can remember her exact words — "Tak it Ella, God's been guid tae us." How the poor can help the poor, with dignity to both the giver and the receiver.

We had another "Uncle" in Edinburgh who came to visit us from time to time. He was in fact the brother-in-law of my grandfather and, despite this and his membership of the "Brethren", he loved to laugh and joke with us. His wife was quiet and colourless, with the dogged and closed mind of her beliefs, and they had two daughters, who were both adopted. Uncle Alec was a keen swimmer and he seldom missed a day at the Edinburgh baths. He may have naturally liked to swim or he may have taken up the habit as a young man in order to cool his ardour. Whatever the reason, swimming was the cause of his death, for one day he dived into the baths but failed to surface again, having suffered a heart attack while under the water.

His widow and daughters lived on quietly as before. The girls were now grown-up and both had good jobs in the Civil Service. They wore no make-up of course, although I can still remember the smell of their fur coats and the dreadful dead foxes with the glassy eyes which were a mark of female opulence at the time.

It was after the war that I learned what had happened to the girls. Their mother had lived on until her early eighties, and by the time she died both girls were around the sixty mark. They had never read a newspaper, never listened to the wireless or worn jewellery or lipstick. Now they both blossomed out, heavily made up and jewel-bedecked, with teetering high heels. Off they went to the dancing, to the cinema and even, it was rumoured, to the lounge bars of select hotels. Within months they both had a boy friend, which was not without its complications as each was courting the same man. One sister in fact married the boy friend and they took off for Canada. I don't know what happened to the other sister, but I hope she found happiness.

CHAPTER
TWELVE

The Miners

Almost merging with the seafaring community to the west of us was a very different world. This was mining country around the little towns of Prestonpans and Tranent. There were two pits along the seashore, the Grange and the Links, and both were old, with narrow coal seams, and, as they ran out into the seabed, they were extremely wet and had to be pumped out continually.

If the phrase "the Hungry Thirties" had any meaning, it was in the colliery villages of England and Scotland at this time. The whole area depended on the pits, and even the output of the brickworks in the colliery yard was regulated by the amount of activity in winning coal.

Summertime was the worst time in the mining communities, for then the demand for coal fell to its low. Unemployment benefit was only for the luckier men and lasted for six months only, and dozens of families were on poor law relief: the "means test" with all its indignities, the humiliations and the sense of being spied on, that this implied. Even by our own poor standards, the poverty was frightening. There was a cinema in Prestonpans where one could get in for tuppence, and from the age of nine or so I would sometimes walk along the shore, the four miles from our village, to go there when I had the cash. Many of the children were ragged and without shoes even in cold weather. They would stand in the matinée queue with one foot on top of the other, changing it round and trying to keep some warmth in the toes.

We were used to poverty in our village. It held few terrors for us, but this was not the quiet poverty of the farms; this was the crowded poverty of a town, and even as a small child it frightened me.

There was a brighter side to this, although I was too young to appreciate it. My older sisters, when they left our junior school and went to the high school in Prestonpans, came into contact with it much more. This was a very real sense of common solidarity which these mining communities had. They shared their adversity and the miners even shared what work there was, so that often it was possible for a workmate to go down the pit long enough to accumulate enough stamps on his card to go back on the "Buroo" and, for a time at least, get off the hated means test.

One of the things the unemployed miners relied on was the age-old custom of gleaning from the fields once the crops had been harvested. In the old days this had meant the odd ears of barley which remained amongst the stubble, but in my day it was mainly potatoes which had been covered by the soil or slit by the blades of the "howker". To a lesser extent it also meant such things as carrots and turnips rejected for harvesting if they were too misshapen for marketing. There was no legal right, of course, but gleaming was an accepted custom, and accepted by both sides, as it effectively cleaned the fields for the next crop. It was a common sight then to see both men and women scouring the harvested fields, as it was common also to see them searching the pit bings for tiny lumps of coal which had escaped the washer. These and the "sea coal", the lumps washed ashore by the tide from the bings which ran out to sea, were bagged and carried home on old bicycles with the chains missing and sometimes the tyres as well, or on battered prams or home-made barrows. It was all a means of existing, and to families on the brink of starvation the gleaning was precious.

A new farmer took over the tenancy of Meadowmill, which was the very large farm on the outskirts of Prestonpans, and he let it be known that anyone found gleaning on his land would be reported to the police. The fields in these Lothian farms are large, often twenty acres or more, and in one of these he had a crop of very fine young cabbage. One morning, in the most mysterious fashion, every single cabbage had been pulled up by the roots. This must have taken the night-time efforts of about a hundred people, but no-one saw a thing. Happily for the peace of mind of the local "polis", concerned as local police are with leading a quiet life, the farmer got the message and gleaning recommenced at Meadowmill.

The speech of the miners and their families was almost as distinctive as that of the fisher folk, and for some obscure reason they insisted on addressing everyone of whatever age, sex or social station as "Sir". Even when squaring up for a fight, small boys would issue the ritual threats with the obligatory "Sir". "I'll belt yer heid in, Sir." It gave their speech a comical overtone which I have never forgotten. The miners needed to laugh; it was about the only thing they could afford. The other, despite their mutual poverty, was a fairly strong current of religious bigotry. A couple of generations back, the Catholic Irish had come into the pits, some in search of any sort of work and some deliberately brought in by the masters to scab during strikes. It had left a legacy of antagonism and bitterness which has not been dissipated to this day.

There were still separate gangs in the pits under Protestant and Catholic contractors, although the Irish were slowly proving to be as militant in the union as the Scots. The Orange lodges were strong and paraded with their bowler hats, banners and ticky-toed walk, every twelfth of July. It was indeed reputed that at Prestonpans an ancient green ham was carried aloft on a pole with a ticket attached which proclaimed that it had been cured at Lourdes. There were even separate clubs for Protestant and Catholic pigeon fanciers, and what were referred to as "Fenian doos" were not encouraged to complete with their Protestant counterparts.

In politics, however, both Orange and Green were solid Labour, except for the few who voted Communist. In both Prestonpans and Tranent, the town on the hill above, the "Cooncil" was composed entirely of Labour members. Although it was the socialism of extreme poverty, a kind of municipal socialism was the result. The co-operative store of course reigned supreme, but in Tranent even the local chip shop was a municipal enterprise, controlled by the Labour Party.

Bitter memories still remained of the great lock-out in 1926. This extended to those who had scabbed during the strike and to the non-miners who had failed to respond to the miners' call for support during the General Strike. Some little businesses had staked their all in giving the miners' families what credit they could during the strike, and they were never forgotten. There was one man called Terry Wiles who ran a little garage and bus service in the mining villages. Terry was an Englishman and he was by trade a mechanic. He was never in his office, but always to be found beneath the bonnet of some vehicle or underneath a bus. He never wore overalls, but a tweed suit which was encrusted with oil, and he was loved by all who knew him. During the day, his three buses ran a shuttle service between Tranent, Port Seton and Prestonpans and the other mining communities around. In the summer evenings he hired out buses for tours and runs, and on speculation one time he announced a great evening mystery tour to Peebles, price half-a-crown.

Terry had carried the miners for nothing during the strike and almost bankrupted himself in the process, but he had cast his bread upon the waters. A few years later, the big bus companies started a price war which, by selective undercutting of fares, was effectively to drive all the local services into the ground: all, that is, except Wiles Motor Buses, for despite the fare-cutting the miners and their families stuck to using Terry's buses and eventually he was left to carry on the routes on his own.

Every town has some sort of a reputation and Tranent's was for jokes. It was only in Tranent that a man could buy a scarf at the co-operative store and take it back the following day because it was too tight. The phrase "Ower ticht" is much more descriptive but not of course universally understood.

Even today Tranent can hardly be called a lovely little town, and in the 1930s the story went around that a newspaper, for first prize in one of its competitions, was offering a week's free holiday for two in Tranent. The runner-up would receive a fortnight's free holiday for two in Tranent. In later life I did in fact know a man who came from Tranent and who made a very good living around the clubs as a stand-up comic, using the fund of Tranent jokes which he had carefully collected and classified in a little notebook he always carried with him.

Sadly, much is lost in the translation but, as other jokes so often centre around characters called Pat and Mike, Tranent comedy was enacted by two miners known as Jock and Eck. Walking along the street, Jock would meet Eck leading a goat. "My Goad, Eck sir", Jock would exclaim, "what the hell are ye daen wi' that goat?" "A hae bocht it," Eck would reply, "an' a'll keep it fur its mulk." "But whaur wull ye keep it, Eck, sir?"

"A'll keep it under the bed." "Whit about the smell, sir?" "Och, goats dinnae min' the smell."

Our excursions to these surrounding towns and villages were few, and usually we walked there. As a rule there would be a reason for our visits. The dentist was in Tranent. The cinema was at Prestonpans. The swimming gala was at Port Seton, and from time to time a rather tired and flea-blown circus felt it worthwhile to pitch its tent at one of these locations.

A circus of sorts actually came to Longniddry once, but it was the poorest of the poor. The tattered little tent was pitched in a clearing near the railway, romantically known as the "Dungly", and only a collection was made instead of a regular admission charge. The proceeds were claimed to go to unemployed miners, but I think this was a ploy to get around the law. All circuses are rather sad, but even to us children, ragged and scruffy as so many of us were, such defeated people could seem pitiful. Still it was entertainment, and entertainment was what we were constantly looking for.

Itinerant singers were common enough and attracted little attention from us, but musicians were worth following, especially the ragged kilted pipers who would come in bands of four or five together. The odd Sikh pedlar with his turban was always followed around the village by a group of little boys making rude comments about "Ghandi" until, driven to desperation, the Sikh would put down his case and pelt us with enough stones to keep us at a respectful distance. "Aw Mr Ghandi", we would sing, "in yer wee dish cloot, dis yer mother ken ye're oot, ye daft galoot; onybody wad think ye were aff för a dook [swim]; ye wad look much better in a plus four suit."

Breton onion hawkers were a much more common sight. They came on bicycles, festooned with strings of their lovely onions. "Ingin Johnny, Ingin Johnny", we would cry. "Wash yir face and you'll look bonny, Comb yir hair wi' the leg o' a chair, Ingin Johnny, Ingin Johnny."

CHAPTER
THIRTEEN

Airships and
Aeroplanes

Despite the universal depression, change was coming to the village. Every so often there would be a droning sound in the air and small children would run about shouting "an aeroplane, an aeroplane". Once we saw a great cigar-shaped object in the sky — an airship, the R34 I think it was, on a proving run from its hangar at East Fortune. This would be shortly before its disastrous voyage to India, which had scarcely commenced before it crashed in flames in France.

Once a plane actually made a forced landing in a field at the home farm, and half the village came to see this wonderful contraption of canvas and wires and hickory with the great wooden propeller. It was shortly after that, one summer about 1935 I think, that some entrepreneur actually started five-bob flights from the sands at Port Seton, where there was a holiday camp. The plane carried four passengers, and of course the fare was a sum beyond our wildest dreams but, rather like the man who danced with a girl who'd danced with the Prince of Wales, I knew a youth who had been given five shillings as a birthday present and who was determined to spend it on the aeroplane flight. We all walked along the beach at low tide and waited for this young man who, already rich beyond the dreams of avarice, arrived on his almost new bicycle, a "racer" of the dropped handlebar variety. He entered the plane, which taxied along the sand and took off. So intent were we on the performance that we failed to notice a thief who calmly rode off on the bike which the youth had propped up against a rock. Looking down from his seat in the plane, the youth himself saw the theft but of course could do nothing about it, and on coming to earth a few minutes later he walked back to the village with us, a sadder and poorer man.

The flotsam of the Great Depression was with us everywhere. It was at Port Seton that I saw a large American negro playing an old guitar for pennies. I had none to give, of course, but I stood beside him long enough to pick up the words of one song, an air which no doubt would be laughed at today as something out of *Uncle Tom's Cabin*, but which I thought was beautiful: "Carry me back to old Virginny, that's the place where the sweet potatoes grow. That's where the birds are a-singin' in the springtime. That's where this darkie's ever longin' for to go. That's where I laboured so hard for Old Massa. Long hours each day in the fields of yellow corn. No place on earth do I long for more sincerely, than old Virginny, the place where I was born." The singer had probably been paid off some ship at Leith and wandered down the coast making a living of sorts.

Less talented were the other detritus who lived in the woods and covert holes around us. These people might by romantics be given the appellation of hermits, but to us they were just people who somehow managed an existence without the endless perambulations to which most tramps were consigned.

Jock Dunbar lived in an old lime-burner's kiln about two miles from our village. He was a quiet and gentle man and we seldom saw him. We respected his cave-like dwelling with sacks hung over the front, and we never intruded on his poor privacy. Coming back over the fields from some ploy in the gloaming, we could see the glow of a candle and the light of Jock's fire. He was found, still in death, by some farmworkers one morning, and all that was left in the old kiln was some sacks and a few boxes. He lived alone and he died alone.

Less reclusive were the two old women who lived quite near the village in a wood. Their home was in a hollow bauk beneath a great tree stump and, since they both had a thirst, they would call at the village grocer's as often as finances would allow. Both of them smoked a pipe, the old clay "cutty" with the stem broken off so that it almost rested on the chin. For their cash they would make and sell clothes pegs around the doors, and through this and the odd begging they managed to get a drink and a smoke. "Ha, Hi Mary, how's Black Sarey?" we would shout after them, this being their respective names, and they would feebly try to chastise us. They were both incredibly filthy, and God knows what rheumatic pains they suffered from in these wet and dripping dark woods. They spent but little of their pittance on food, because they could glean potatoes and even barley from the fields, and with a box of matches they could get by.

Of course many of the people we thought of as very old were, by today's standards, not even middle-aged. The hermits, and the beggars who came to the village either on their regular rounds or as drifters, certainly included some quite young people, but poverty and defeat, and often booze as well, had aged them all.

Even "respectable" people, however, if they were working-class, aged quickly. This was especially true of women. A diet high in carbohydrates and low in protein quickly turned most women to fat but, in any event, no wife of a working man with a family could afford to dress decently or to have her hair dressed, or even to look after her teeth. At forty, then, wives were already tired and old and drab, and they accepted this as their fate. They even managed to have some measure of contempt for the only women who contrived to stay smart in their appearance, almost invariably the spinsters who were presumed incapable of "getting a man".

Since we had no pub, the village grocer sold beer by the bottle and spirits, which had to be consumed in the backyard, if not at home. During the harvest season on a Saturday there would often be a small group of Irish labourers here, buying the provisions for the coming week. The stereotype of the drunken Irish did not apply to these men and to the few girls who came with them. They were mostly Donegal men, across to get enough money during the season so that they could pay the rent at home for the rest of the year. We might be poor, but they managed to live on practically nothing for the three months or so they were in Scotland. They were mainly Irish-speaking, some still wearing the "baneen" jackets, and they lived on potatoes with a little bacon and some milk. The odd loaf of bought bread or jar of cheap jam was a luxury, and I have often seen a grown man buy a halfpenny packet of sweets for himself as probably his one indulgence of a week's back-breaking work.

These travelling workers would move from farm to farm, first building the stooks when the oats and barley were harvested, then starting on the potatoes and working until late October or early November. "Wha saw the tattie howkers?" we would sing. "Wha saw them ga'n awe? Wha saw the tattie howkers, sailin' down the Broomielaw? Some o' them had bits an' grevits, some o' them had nane at a', some o' them had umberellis, for tae keep the rain awa'." Most of the tattie howkers sailed away down the Broomielaw after the harvest and back to Donegal, but some always stayed in Scotland. Many became drifters, working on any sort of casual labour while their strength lasted, without roots and drunken when the money was there. The warmth of a pub and the glow from booze could be a welcome alternative to a life spent in bothies, huts and dossers. Some of the Irish married, however, and their second generation are all over the Lothian countryside today, mixed with the native Scots and the descendants of those earlier itinerant farmworkers who came to the Lowlands each year from the Gaelic-speaking western Highlands.

The farms were all around us but, to village children, they were places of adventure and excitement, and as the opportunity offered, places were we could earn some casual money. To this extent therefore we viewed the farms as outsiders rather than, as the farmworkers did, the centre of our everyday lives.

The barley harvest was perhaps the most exciting time of all for young children. This was still the age of the horsedrawn reaper binder. The tractor had scarce made an appearance and the combine harvester had not yet been heard of. Word would go around that such-and-such a field near the village would be ready to cut, and all the village boys would congregate with a stick in the one hand and a stone in the other. The man with the scythe would first come in and cut a swathe round the edge of the field, wide enough to let the reaper in, and as the workers stacked the sheaves into stooks, the boys would follow the reaper, all eyes on the hem of the barley stalks as they were bent on to the cutter by the whirling arms of the binder.

Soon the first rabbit would bolt out from the field, to be followed by a hail of stones and flailing sticks. Some rabbits were killed, but most got away. The high spot of excitement, however, was when the reaper moved in to cut the last triangle of grain. Here there would be as many as half-a-dozen rabbits, driven into the ever-diminishing shelter of the centre of the field by the whirling arms of the reaper and the noise.

The fields cut and stooked, the stooks made ideal playhouses, where the girls could bring their dolls and the boys could pretend they were Red Indians in wigwams.

The boys of course had secret and more important houses, deep in the woods or down by the seashore. These were the centre of "gangs", the membership of which was constantly changing as new alliances were forged or the age of admittance was reached, or the acquisition of long trousers compelled the resignation of senior members. Some gang houses were built on the branches of trees, although none too successfully, as this required both techniques and materials in which we were deficient. I loved climbing trees and had done so even when my father was alive. He had prohibited this and had once belted me when he passed on his bike and saw me swaying on a branch about ten feet above the ground. Mother made me promise not to climb trees, but I couldn't resist the temptation and I continued the vice in secret. Soon there was not a tree, no matter how tall, in the village that I hadn't climbed right to the top. I was both agile and light and most branches would support me. I would cross over from one tree to another when the branches were close enough. It was a sensation of excitement mixed with fear, to be at the swaying top of a tall tree, looking down on the world, especially if I had climbed secretly and alone. I suppose it was fortunate that I never fell and injured myself. One boy less agile than me did fall, fortunately not from a great height, but high enough to break his leg.

We walked along the tops of walls, and I could even walk along the tops of wire fences using a sort of tightrope technique. There was almost no traffic on the roads, of course, especially around the farm lanes, but we boys ran all sorts of dangers and hazards.

We would make explosives of a sort by mixing carbide, which provided the light for early bicycle lamps, with water, shaking it and sealing it in a tin. This tin was then thrown away and within a few seconds it would blow apart. We would also lie across logs in the sunlight in deep water-filled quarries and snare eels with a "girn", a fine wire snare. We would make crazy contraptions of old oil barrels and driftwood lashed together, and with these we would launch ourselves out into the open sea.

Our activities varied with the seasons. In the winter, every boy had his "firecan". I haven't seen a firecan for many years now, but what fun and excitement they held for us in the winter nights. The firecan was an ordinary tin which we pierced full of holes with a rock and an old nail. A syrup tin was the best, and in consequence in short supply, for the removable lid meant that it had a strong rim. The rim was pierced in two places and a loop of wire was formed to fasten at the holes, making a handle about eighteen inches long. We would leave home after scrounging or stealing a match; I never used the door of our house, always leaving or entering through a window, and we would meet in groups, usually near the station.

We would start the fires in our cans, using a little newspaper or grass and some dry twigs; then we would sneak onto the railway siding near where the engines were coaled, and here we would pick up tiny lumps of coal and ash. Now we could whirl the firecans around our heads or in patterns from side to side, or changing arms, until the coals glowed. We could then move off to a field of late potatoes or to the end of a clamp where, in the dark, we could conduct a raid so that each firecan held a large potato which could be roasted and eaten. Sometimes someone with some foresight had even managed to bring a little salt. The potatoes of course were burned black on the outside and half raw on the inside, but we ate them nonetheless and swore they were "the haws" or, as the English would say, excellent. We could then spend the rest of the evening roaming through the village, admiring the patterns of light our whirling firecans made until, tired and sooty with blackened mouths from the potatoes, we drifted off to our homes.

CHAPTER
FOURTEEN

Winter and Spring

Winter was the time for the "bool" season. Every boy would suddenly be seen to be carrying an old sock or even a specially made bag, each holding his collection of marbles. These would be of several kinds and degrees of importance. The tiny clay ones, the "peeps", were made mainly to be won or lost when the serious gaming for "keepies" began. Next were the stoneware "jarries", which were the workhorses of marble playing. Then there were the "glassies". These were beauties, made to be admired or even, in the case of special examples, exchanged for as many as half a dozen of the inferior kind. Some of the glass marbles were beautiful creations of swirling colours within the clear glass, and the finest of these were known to us all, to be taken out of the bag, admired and displayed. The really fearsome "bools", however, were the "steelies", the steel ballbearings which were heavy and could crash and roll into rival marbles with devastating effect. So fearsome was the reputation of some of these that they were banned from use in many of our games.

We played on the usual basis of knocking rival marbles out of a circle, and to do this it was obligatory to "knuckle" or propel the bool, using the knuckle of the thumb and the forefinger only. We also played "kellie", which involved digging a series of holes in the ground about three inches deep and four inches across, into which we tried to knuckle the bools.

It is surprising now to think how much of our time, even on cold winter nights, we spent out of doors. Many of our games would be played under a lamp-post, and often under the same post there would be a little group of boys playing their bools and three or four little girls playing their complicated games of skipping, to which boys were never admitted. When I was very small, the village had wooden lamp-posts with iron cages at the top, with oil lamps which were lit and trimmed every night by a man who went his rounds with a long pole and who always stank of paraffin. Just about the time father died, electricity came to most of the village, the lamps became brighter and were on top of poles made of cast iron. Here was a ready-made swing and free light into the bargain. "Peevers", or what the English call hopscotch, was usually a girls' game and was full of the recondite rules in which little girls seem to delight. Very often, it seemed to me, most of these female games would be spent in arguing or discussing the interpretation of some rule, with much finger-pointing and arm-waving. But this was the way of females, and we accepted it as only a vague irritant, as it went on beside us in the circle of light.

There was little danger from passing cars and we could freely run into the road. At the same time, mothers knew where we were, and often indeed they could see their children under their favourite lamp-post, so big sisters and brothers could be sent to fetch us home at bedtime.

Certain games were for boys and others were for girls, but a winter night's game which we all played was "kick the can". Here a tin can was placed under the lamp-post and the one who was "het", or "it" in English, kicked it as hard as she or he could. Meanwhile the others went to hide in the darkness. The can was recovered and guarded by the "het", but we would then make sudden rushes and if anyone was not touched, they could in turn kick the can and become "het". Who was to be the "het" at the commencement of each game was determined by a process of counting out, itself the source of further argument. "Oor wee Jeanie has a nice new peenie and guess what colour it was." At the word "was" the person would say a colour, perhaps "Broon". Nothing daunted, the enumerator would count, "B. R. O. O. N. spells Broon and O. U. T. spells OUT." Simpler and just as popular was, "I think, I think, I smell a stink, coming from I. O. U."

When the weather was really cold and frosty we made slides which were the terror of pedestrians and the despair of parents, who made us promise not to use the slides, since they wore out our boots so quickly. Another thing we boys were forbidden to do was to strike our tackety soles along the stones of the road so that they made sparks in the dark. When father was alive, he had mended our boots — for the girls then wore boots too — on his cobbler's last, but now the last was silent and I can still see the look of despair on mother's face as she held out my boots in her hand and looked at the scuffed soles.

The ponds froze in prolonged hard weather, and once the laird even let the village into his estate where the ornamental ponds were frozen hard and the affluent skated around on real skates to the music of a gramophone with a big horn. It was with frosts like these that the margins of the sea froze, and the water in the pools among the rocks. We would go down to look at this wonder and watch the pack ice coming in on the tide. This sea ice had a dirty yellow tinge and it was not slippery like the fresh water ice, so one could run across the pools quite quickly. We would beg a match and light a fire from the driftwood and make believe we were Arctic explorers caught in the search for the North-West Passage.

Autumn was a milder season, and its onset was marked by the chestnut-playing time. We never used the English word "conkers" to describe this game, but we played it with dedication and enthusiasm. Our real fun, however, was in getting the chestnuts from the trees, for we could never wait until they had ripened sufficiently to fall to the ground. We would spend hours throwing sticks up into the branches to shake them off, and as a horse chestnut is a very difficult tree to climb, my special skills were in great demand.

Autumn too was the time for bramble picking. We looked on this at least partly as pleasure but, apart from the fact that mother made great quantities of bramble jelly, we could often sell a large part of our pickings to add to the family budget and save up for such treats as a bus ride and a visit to the pantomime in Edinburgh. Mushrooms grew in profusion around the village, especially in one field, but I knew of no-one who would eat them except "Daddy" Bell the engine driver, who drove the "Haddington Express", the little train which was the only one to run back and forth daily on the five-mile track to Haddington.

"Cock Dinty" required no specialised equipment, as it was a game which depended wholly on the ability to hop about on one leg. The idea was to fold one's arms and to remain balanced on the one foot while hopping and dodging, or "joukin", and to crash into one's opponent so as to make him retrieve his balance by putting his other leg on the ground. With a good sense of balance and, being agile, this was a game which I enjoyed and at which I excelled.

I enjoyed making and flying my own kites. Nowadays one can just go and buy a kite made of plastic, but there is little fun in flying something which you haven't made yourself.

I would cut a couple of light hazel rods, a long one and a shorter one, and cross-tie the shorter rod about two-thirds along the length of the longer one. I would then tightly tie string along the outside of the rods, making a frame. The covering of the kite could then be made by glueing brown paper over the completed frame. The thicker end of the hazel should always be at the foot of the kite and a mooring string should be fastened loosely along the shorter length of the frame. A "tail" could easily be made by attaching folded lengths of newspaper at intervals, to another piece of string fastened to the foot of the kite. This was for balance, and the correct length of the tail was achieved by trial and error, or *in extremis* and in a gale, by attaching a divot of grass to the tail's end. By a process of continual scrounging, enough string could be procured to fly the kite, and with success and suitable cadging this string could be lengthened. If there was no glue for the kite's construction, then a paste of flour and water would suffice.

Every boy had a "gird", which the English called a hoop. At school we had a poetry book with several poems by A. A. Milne which showed the illustrations of pretty little middle-class English boys playing with their hoops. To us they might as well have been Hottentots, so far were they removed from our experience. Our girds were made from old bicycle wheels with the spokes removed. It was very necessary to remove the spokes, for when the gird had gathered speed it could be maintained and guided by simply pressing the stick we all used for this purpose into the groove in the centre, where once the bicycle tyre had fitted.

We also used old motor-car tyres as girds. These were much narrower than today's tyres, and it was even possible to increase their speed by a sort of flywheel effect, using a couple of old billiard balls inside the tyre. I have even seen some enterprising larger boys persuade a gullible or reckless child to actually balance sitting inside the tyre while it was propelled downhill. This took courage or stupidity of a high order, as I discovered on my one and only trip, which ended in scraped shins and a large bump on my forehead.

Some of the luckier boys had a "guider", a barrow usually fitted with old pram wheels with a front end which could be steered. Pram wheels were, however, a rare luxury, as indeed were prams in our village, and we constantly scoured the village midden for specimens which, when we did find them, were invariably buckled and missing some spokes. The middens yielded other and usually nameless treasures, especially from the contents of the middle-class houses by the sea, which were rumoured to throw away their toys from the previous year before the advent of a fresh Christmas.

We made our own entertainment, but there were some spectator sports and the chief of these was at the village weddings. No working-class wedding was complete without a "poor oot", or the throwing of a handful of pennies to the watching children. The middle-class weddings were without this largesse, and we never bothered to attend them in consequence. Theirs was the luxury, ours was the fun.

Our greatest and everlasting delight, however, was the sea. Our beach was not too sandy and the rocky reefs and pools made it an endless place of fascination for children. Perhaps the greatest mistake that parents can make is to take their children on holiday to a wide sandy beach. Sand is fine, and so is the water, but after digging and paddling they soon pall.

Rocks and pools are entirely different. Here are small fish and crabs and sea anemones and seaweed and mussels and limpets and whelks and places to dive in deep water or to fish from or to watch the seals bask on lonely days.

Rocky beaches yield flotsam of all sorts and firewood in abundance, and on such beaches, where few people venture, great driftwood fires can be lit without interference.

Beaches even yield food from the rocks in the form of mussels and buckies, the latter being, I think, "winkles" in English. We particularly liked the buckies, as they could be eaten without salt and the culinary utensils were all at hand. We would get an old tin from the tideline and fill it full of buckies of the largest kind. These could be got by the gallon from the sides of the rocks and there was little or no danger of pollution in those days. We then went to a freshwater spring, of which there were several which ran out onto the beach, and we washed the buckies clean of sand. These were then boiled in spring water on a fire of driftwood, and we would extract them from their shells with a large thorn from the buckthorn thickets which grew all along the beach. We made tea as well, without milk but with plenty of sugar, and if we found the odd potato on the beach, we boiled that as well.

We were all well fed at home, at least within the limits of what mother could afford, but we lived as much as possible out of doors and we ate what we could as we found it and in season. There were red currants on two secret bushes amongst the sand dunes

112

down by the sea, and here there was also a large and prolific gooseberry bush. Gooseberries could also be found in profusion by walking down the course of an overgrown burn: again a secret discovery, which only I and my sisters knew of. Brambles of course grew everywhere but we, as a family with our keen commercial instinct, knew of all the best places.

We never ate mushrooms cooked, but we peeled them and ate them raw, and we would take an odd turnip, a "neep", from the fields and knock off the root on a wire fence and then tear the skin off with our teeth. The delightful taste of fresh turnip mingled with the taste of fresh earth on an October morning is with me yet. The taking of turnips from the edge of the fields and the "mumping" of a few potatoes for our firecans was accepted, at least by us, as custom and we did not consider it to be stealing. In other respects, although there were fields of peas and strawberries and rasps, we would never consider eating any except, as was our right, during the picking season if we were working there.

Mother's love of flowers led us to a tortuous self-justification on occasion. We had lovely roses in our ruin of a garden but the display of flowers of other sorts, since father's death, had sadly diminished. We therefore manipulated ourselves into the belief that flowers which hung over a garden fence and onto the footpath were no longer really private property but, somehow or other, had cast themselves into the wild. Thus justified, we would carry home hastily plucked bunches of chrysanthemums to mother, until at length she convinced us we were doing wrong.

It certainly was no wrong, however, to pick the primroses and the violets from the woods and this we did with enthusiasm, but with expertise as well, every spring. Along the railway line to Haddington was a great beech wood which in April was carpeted deep in primroses. These grew on the railway cutting outside the wood as well and, since there were no trains on a Sunday, we could safely walk along the track to the wood. We carried baskets and reels of thread, for we were professionals who first filled our own house with primroses and then made a market for so many bunches at a halfpenny each.

Mother had been a florist in her youth and she showed us how to pick the stems, nipping them off right at the base with our finger and thumbnail, and always taking flowers which were just coming out from the bud. We would arrange some leaves to set off each bunch and these would be laid gently in the basket until we had several dozen. No-one minded our picking, and I am sure that the quantities of primroses were so vast that it made not the slightest difference to their future growth. We picked only to the limit of our restricted market and we would never cast aside a single flower, once picked.

Mother had a reverence for all flowers and she showed us how to treat them with respect. She would be aghast at seeing someone with a bunch of flowers wrapped in newspaper. "My goodness," she would exclaim, as if she had seen a naked belly dancer, "I saw this woman with a fur coat and, what do you think" — she would pause to let her words have their full impact — "She was carrying a bunch of flowers wrapped in newspaper." The full horror of mother's reaction is with me yet.

The laird had great banks of daffodils in front of the "Big Hoose" and once, when I was about six, I could not resist the temptation to "loup" the "dyke", or the wall, and gather an armful for mother. He had so many, they would never be missed, and I was so small that I was not seen but, due to fear or mother's admonition or the risk of being found out and reported to Mr. Mackay the "polis", in future years I left the laird's daffodils alone.

We had few wild raspberries in or around the village, but wild strawberries grew in profusion. The favourite place for these was along the same railway line where we went for the primroses and in secret water-filled quarries in a pine wood. These were old limestone quarries where the rock had been extracted and burned in the kilns years before, when the farmland was being sweetened and recovered from the bogs. Now old Jock Dunbar lived in the abandoned kilns and deep and clear water had entered the three quarries from underground springs.

In later years we all went swimming in these quarries, and the margins yielded a variety of exotic plants which found the limestone congenial to their growth. So also of course did the wild strawberries and we could pick the tiny, bittersweet berries by the basket here. We ate them where we picked them, and we ate them at home, and mother made a strong jam from them, but no-one in the village would buy them.

A few years after the War I took my own two little children to this lovely and secluded spot. The entire pinewood had been cut down, but the quarries were still there and we picked the strawberries once more. Several years ago I went back once more, by myself now, as my children had long grown up. The quarries were now a rubbish dump of ashes and tin cans and old soap packets, with a few brackish pools and a smell of filth and decay. The magic had gone for ever.

FIFTEEN

Hallowe'en; Christmas; Sunday School Picnics

To a very large extent our festivals, such as they were, remained Scottish, although with our increasing anglicisation things were slowly changing. This was Calvinist Lowland Scotland, where the pubs shut on Sunday along with all the cinemas, theatres and most shops. To get a drink, a working man (for the rich had their clubs) had to travel a minimum of three miles and sign a book with his name and address, to show that he was a "bona fide" traveller. He then had to buy a meal, or at least something to eat, at the few hotels which had this parody of a licence for Sunday opening. A pie would be the favourite item necessary to comply with the law, and once bought it could either be eaten or discounted against future drink, until it had passed through so many hands that, weary with its life, it fell apart.

So it was that we had no Easter, but we had a holiday on Lammas and Martinmas. Nor did we know of Advent or Lent, although Christmas itself was creeping in. Christmas was increasingly held as a time for present-giving, but it was a children's festival only. Even then, some children got their treat at New Year, which was the real Scottish festival time. Christmas Day was an ordinary working day, and shops remained open as usual.

We children had a routine within the family for Christmas which never seemed to vary. We would start around September with a determination to save up and a panicky feeling that Christmas was near. We would each exploit our little "seam" to raise cash, and in my case I would even start knocking on the doors of people with no children who occasionally employed me to run a "message" to the post office or the shop and I would actually tout for business. Picking brambles and selling them was another method and, of course, before the playing field was laid out, I could always earn at least sixpence in the mushroom season by picking supplies for "Daddy" Bell.

The tips from our milk and paper rounds, however, were our main source of Christmas income, and since these were given perilously near to Christmas itself, our Christmas shopping was always a last-minute affair. Fortunately our gift lists were simple. As a family we were all passionately fond of chocolate, and plain cream Fry's chocolate in particular. This included mother, who always contrived somehow to eat one square of Fry's cream when she went to bed each night and with it, if she could at all manage, a half orange.

We would usually club together therefore and buy mother plain chocolate, and I would buy my sisters chocolate as well. For a shilling it was possible to buy a "selection box" containing six bars of Fry's cream, each of a different flavour — vanilla, raspberry, coffee, mint, lemon and orange. If funds allowed, I would present these to each of my sisters and, as often as not, they would give the same to me. Sometimes funds would not stretch all the way to a shilling each, but we still contrived as a rule to present each other with enough chocolate to make all of us feel satisfyingly sick for the better part of a week. As the girls got older and started working more, the delights of Woolworths sixpenny and threepenny store in Edinburgh would exert their annual spell and Christmas shopping would to a large extent be transferred to the endless permutations of rubbish, mainly from Japan, destined to fall apart in the course of a few weeks.

Hallowe'en, or All Hallows Eve, was the second most important time for children. Here we had "dooking" for nuts and apples in a basin of water and our games and parties. It was a chance, too, to make some money, for we went out "guising" in any old and weird costume that we could put together, with blackened faces and turnip lanterns cut into the shape of fierce faces illuminated with a guttering and smelly candle.

We "chapped" on the village doors in gangs of three or four and we were expected to say our party piece or to sing a song, and then it was "please to help the guisers", with either a door shut firmly in our faces or an apple or an orange or a penny or two. At the end of our evening's work the cashier amongst us would divide the spoils, which could amount to as much as sixpence each. More fabled sums had been heard of, but they never came our way. Once more it was the working-class houses in the village which contributed, and by bitter experience we had discovered that the middle classes were a waste of time. This was true also of the small tips we received at Christmas or, more often, around New Year, from our milk and paper rounds. A very few houses left two pennies or a thrupenny bit with the cook at the back door, but those who could afford the most gave the least or, more often, nothing at all.

Fireworks were on sale, but those of us who could afford to spend a halfpenny on a squib or a penny on a rocket usually let them off as soon as they were bought, or waited impatiently until it was at least half dark. Bonfires too were for Hallowe'en or Hogmanay. The first of April was "Hunt the Gowk" or practical joke time, but only until mid-day. Holidays, or at least holidays away from home, were even for the more prosperous something almost unheard of, although a few families would go to such unlikely spots as Motherwell or Airdrie, to stay with relatives in return for hospitality at our seaside village.

Most of us went to Sunday school. Most of us, that is, from the village, but few from the farms. Even the McVeighs with their curious religious background went there, partly because mother, despite her reservations about the Established Church, thought it must be good for us, and partly for other reasons. Like other mothers, it gave her some peace on a Sunday morning. For our part we went there, neither out of a very profound religious conviction nor from a desire for theological knowledge, but because twice a year, once during the winter at the church hall, and once during the summer by charabanc, we had church "treats".

The catering for these treats was simple. Each child was given a bag of buns and drew as many cups of tea as he or she wanted from a big copper urn. There would be six buns in the bag, and the top two would be best as they had icing on them. As one went down the bag, so one went down the scale of attraction via the doughnuts to the scones at the foot.

We played unaccustomed and anglicised games like "the farmer's in his den", passing the parcel and musical chairs, and each child who had a party piece was called on to perform. The McVeighs were, of course, always to the fore in anything dramatic and nothing was too ambitious or too maudlin for us to tackle. Mother loved poetry in the long and declamatory late Victorian style of her girlhood, and we had two epics which each of the girls performed in turn as they grew older. They inherited the right to perform these poems as an old coat would be passed from sister to sister.

We loved to perform these poems on our Sunday walks, for they were poems which had to be performed as well as spoken or, rather, declaimed. Our other great family dramatic effort was a joint production of *Uncle Tom's Cabin* in which I, being the smallest, was always cast as Topsy and Marion, being an adept bullier, always became Simon Legree.

121

The first of the poems was called "Curfew shall not ring tonight". This was fully 40 verses about a brave and exceptionally stupid girl whose father was condemned to death by Cromwell for some undisclosed piece of treason to the Roundhead cause. Sentence was to be carried out at curfew, and curfew was tolled on the bell of the village church. The daughter accordingly climbed out to the top of the bell tower and, instead of cutting the bell rope or wrapping the clapper in cloth as anyone with a grain of sense would have done, she held on like grim death to the clapper of the bell as the bellringer pulled on the rope. The old bellringer was conveniently stone deaf and did not know that the brave but stupid child was swinging above him with bruised knuckles and ringing ears. All ended well, for Cromwell's grim commander had witnessed this feat of endurance and decreed that any father who had brought a child like that into the world deserved to live.

We knew nothing of Scottish poetry or the Scottish literary tradition. My grandfather sang one secular song, and he sang it well. It was called "The Yeomen of England". "Who are the yeomen," he would ask, and answer himself: "The yeomen are the freemen, the freemen of England. Strong were their bows when they went out to war. Bright was their courage for the honour of England. And Spaniards and Dutchmen and Frenchmen and such men, As foemen did fear them, the bowmen of England. No other land could nurse them. The yeomen of England. And on her broad bosom, may they ever lie." For our part we were ignorant of the beautiful poem "Caller Herrin", about

122

the fishermen on our own doorstep, and we had learned another of mother's English epics, about the fishermen of Brixham in, of all places, Devon. "The Boats of Brixham" described a sudden storm and the anxious waiting of the families of the fishermen as the boats battled back to the harbour. Kathleen was the acknowledged expert on the delivery of this piece, and before she left us to take up her career as a skivvy she would hold the floor at each Sunday-school party and give us the full treatment. She had a printed copy of the poem and held this in her hand, not because she did not know its every word, but because she considered it more sophisticated to at least pretend to read it. "One by one they staggered homeward," she would intone and flap her arms like a wounded seagull. "Waiting on the quayside," then she would point, jabbing her finger in various directions, "Here a mother, there a son." It was all heady stuff, and as a family we were each other's sternest critics. Marion, with her great comic gifts, always went over in big way. She had an incredible dance which she had acquired from one of the child patients during one of her stays in hospital. This she called the "Hullicky Dulky" dance (my spelling is, as hers was, phonetic). There was a song to the dance, which went: "Hullicky Dulky, Hullicky Dee, Hullicky Dulky Deary, Hullicky Dulky Hullicky Dee, I wish that I could marry," and a marriage proposal and eventual acceptance were related between vigorous leaps, armstretching and high kicks. Called for an encore, Marion would give the Beadle's song in praise of whisky: "Twelve and a tanner a bottle", staggering

123

about and clutching an empty lemonade bottle at which she took from time to time great gulps, with her head thrown back.

Eventually the party would peter out, and even those children who were so hungry that they would always eat the despised scones at the foot of the bag — theirs and anyone else's — would be ready to go. The back door of the hall would open and, as we went out into the frosty night, we would each be handed an apple and an orange.

In a sense we had paid for our treats, for there was a weekly collection at the Sunday School where, for the smallest, a halfpenny was considered the minimum contribution and a penny gave some sort of prestige, like a new jersey or a pair of trousers.

Our summer treat was the annual "trip", and this always posed a conflict of interests. Our parish was a large one and our village church was subordinate to the main and original church at Gladsmuir although, due to recent growth, our village was much larger in size. Four miles inland was in those days a long way from the sea, and the Gladsmuir children for the most part seldom saw it. For us, of course, the sea was only a few minutes away. The inland children therefore wanted to go to the sea and we wanted to go inland. Funds were not sufficient to organise two trips and therefore we compromised. One year we would go to the seaside and the next we would go to some village in the hills, particularly if there was a common green or a friendly local laird.

These were still the days of the open-topped charabancs with rows of doors down the near side like an old-fashioned railway coach, each with its polished brass handle. We would only travel ten miles or so, but movement was slow, and it was the "hurl", the songs we could sing, the general racket we could create and the streamers we could trail in our wake that mattered. Balloons were much too dear, but a whole packet of six streamers could be bought for a penny and thus an entire family could have enough from this outlay.

The fun consisted largely of races of various kinds and for various ages, both straightforward running and egg-and-spoon and sack races, and of course the three-legged race. All of these generated accusations of cheating, which indeed was rampant. The dominant idea was to win the race and get the prize, usually a bar of chocolate, and if this involved a too early start or loosening of the band for the three-legged race, or finding a convenient hole in the corner of the sack, then the opportunity was, in most cases, exploited to the full.

The same bag of buns and the same tea, this time with the urn boiled over an open fire, completed the catering. Most of us had a penny or at least a halfpenny to spend, and if we were at a village we would make for the village shop. At the seaside there were always vans or barrows from which we bought ice cream. There was a technique in spending the smallest amount of money, which we exploited to the full. For ice cream, a halfpenny could buy a cone, or a "cornet" as we always called it, but a penny could buy a much bigger

125

cornet or a wafer, which we always knew as a "slider". It was only a fool, however, who bought a penny cornet, for we all knew that we got more ice cream if we bought the slider. Raspberry essence was always an option, and since this was free we always took it. We never went away with our purchases without ritually asking the ice cream man if he had any broken wafers, and sometimes we would be lucky enough to get a handful from the foot of the tin. If we had bought a cone, the end would be bitten off and the contents sucked down to the bottom, as it lasted better that way. Sometimes a purchase had to be shared amongst the entire family and, by previous debate, one of my sisters would be delegated as holder and the ice cream would be licked by one and closely watched by the others, but meantime remaining firmly in the grip of the holder.

The choice in the village shops was of course greater but, as this was before the days of freezers, no ice cream was available here. If we had money, we usually asked first of all if there were any broken biscuits. These, when available, were considered a great bargain. They were made up from old and damp and frosted specimens and had a peculiar smell, but we always got a lot for our money and quantity was of supreme importance to us. As for the rest of the stock, the choice was always daunting. Many village shops had a peculiar machine which dispensed drinks via a gas cylinder and bottles of brightly coloured and frightful tasting essences. These were known as "Vantas" drinks and they were extremely sweet and gassy, and they created a series of very satisfying belches as one left the shop.

Whole factories were devoted to the production of cheap sweets for children to buy at a halfpenny and a penny. For the reckless there were "lucky bags". These contained some cheap and usually broken sweets and often a liquorice pod and a small and rubbishy tin toy made in Japan or Germany. There were "lucky potatoes" too, many of which were rumoured to contain a threepenny piece, but most of which once more contained a little tin toy. The "potatoes" were made of cheap candy which easily broke young teeth and were dusted with cocoa. Sticks of this candy were sold in paper rolls which had a picture of a fat policeman with his baton drawn, chasing a little dog along the street. We knew this candy as "Polishman's Gundy".

Then there were "sherbet dabs", which were little triangular-shaped "pokes" of sherbet and fine sugar with a tube of liquorice stuck into the top. The sherbet would be sucked up the tube, and always this caused a fit of coughing, which no doubt was designed to give the feeling of money well spent. I was passionately fond of chocolate, which was sheer folly to buy, but I bought it nevertheless. This was not the kind of chocolate which adults bought in tuppenny and fourpenny bars. We only saw this real chocolate, to eat at least, on Christmas and birthdays. My chocolate was of the cheapest cocoa bean and sugar variety in the form of "chocolate drops". So devoted was I to this concoction that I often thought that when I grew up with unlimited money to spend, I would become addicted to chocolate drops and eventually expire through overeating them.

Toffee lasted longer, and this was of two main kinds, known respectively as "Highland Cream" and "Mountain Maid". These were in penny blocks, wrapped in greased paper, one with a picture of a mountain and one of a dairymaid. This toffee stuck to the teeth, and indeed for young children changing their teeth it often performed the function of a dentist, extracting a loose tooth which became firmly embedded in the chewy mass. We could also buy various kinds of liquorice in sticks and rolls, ready sweetened. A part of this was usually eaten and the rest was taken home to make "Sugar Ally Water".

"Sugar Ally Water, black as the lum, gether up yer peens an ye'll a' get some." We would each contrive to get hold of a bottle with a screw top. It was not so simple to obtain a lemonade bottle, for these were in short supply. There was a whole penny deposit charged on lemonade bottles, and we often spent our afternoons scouring the beaches in summer looking for the odd lemonade bottle which rich picnickers were said to discard with never a second thought.

Our sugar ally water therefore was usually confined to empty sauce bottles or others of the screwtop variety which had held even more mysterious liquids. The idea was to shake the mixture and then put it away in a dark cupboard to mature, but it was not in our natures to leave anything which could be eaten or drunk for very long. Thus small boys could be seen with awkward bulges in their jerseys during a sugar ally water epidemic. These bottles would be extracted, shaken, compared with rival mixtures for colour, and then sampled. Few vintages, if any, lived to maturity and within a few days the bottles were empty and the fever would subside.

CHAPTER
SIXTEEN

The Poachers;
The Swimming Club

Longniddry had three houses standing a little to the west of the main street, and thus they were the first houses to be met with on entering from the direction of Edinburgh. On the right, standing in a narrow strip of land between the road and the railway, was a cottage which must have been there before the railway was built. The London trains thundered by only a few feet away, and it is unlikely that anyone in the brightly lit carriages of the night Pullman ever thought of the lamplit window or realised that, in that leaky old but and ben, there was no sanitation or running water.

A family called Tawse inhabited the cottage. I cannot remember the father, but there were a mother and a daughter and a son. Both mother and daughter had long hair and the daughter was very proud of hers although it was to a moderate but marked degree, like her mother's, lousy. The mother was a film fan who bought one of the cheap film magazines with badly printed pictures of film stars in brown and white and full of breathless details of their romantic lives. For some reason she became convinced that Norah had legs closely resembling those of Marlene Dietrich, and she constantly proclaimed this conviction to the world.

The boy was clever and he obtained a scholarship to the Knox Academy in Haddington. This school had a smartly turned-out cadet corps whose khaki uniforms were issued gratis. The uniform, however, although it included a hat, did not extend to the boots, and I can remember the boy waiting on the platform for the train to Haddington, smartly turned out in khaki with neatly wrapped puttees ending in a pair of broken and toeless boots.

That cottage is gone now, but on the other side of the road the great beech tree still stands where my father once carved my initials, and neatly — like everything my father did with his hands. "P.G. McV." it read, and for years it stood out from all the other poor attempts at name carving on the tree. I cannot make out the initials now, but the two cottages on the other side of the road are still there and still as neat and flower-bedecked as ever. These were roadmen's cottages built by the country council. A roadman's may be a fairly lowly job, but it was not without its prestige in those days, even if it was largely the prestige of steady and pensionable employment.

Mr Morton lived in the first of these cottages and, with Mr Fraser, he started and ran the Longniddry Swimming Club. This was a bold venture for its time and place. Somehow, probably by means of a jumble sale, the initial capital was raised to cement over the rocks at a place which was sandy and where at high tide there was about ten feet of water. A steel ladder was fixed to the rock side, a raft was moored about 25 yards away and a diving board was fitted on the cement-covered rocks. These, with two changing huts, constituted the swimming club, and for a subscription of fourpence for children and sixpence for adults, provided the tide was in and it was summer, we could enjoy the illusion of a swimming pool.

Mr Morton was a dedicated and devoted secretary of the kind that every amateur club needs and he was also a keen swimmer. He was, however, quite bald and very sensitive about this fact. He would therefore go swimming with his cloth cap on his head. His friend and assistant secretary, Mr Fraser, who was the village cobbler, had lost his right leg at the hip during the war. This did not stop him unstrapping his peg leg and hopping along the diving board into the water, then swimming strongly to the raft.

We had one almost legendary swimmer at the Longniddry rocks called Kit Griffin. Kit was an engine driver by occupation and he lived at a cottage at Harelaw, a mile or so to the east of the village.

Summer and winter, day and night, Kit swam when he came off his shift, no matter what the weather. Kit declined to wear a swimming costume but would wear only a sort of pouch at the front so that from the rear, he looked quite naked. Being a modest man, he chose not to swim on good days when there were people about and indeed several busybody ladies, it was said, had at one time made a complaint to the local polis concerning Kit's scandalous appearance which must have thrilled them no end.

132

There are rows of little houses built now on the field behind the beech tree where we weeded the leeks and Gaga Allen would belt me on the backside for only using one hand, but a few of the plum trees from the far orchard still stand amongst the houses. These were old and fabled Victoria plums, reputed to be supplied to the royal family when they stayed at the Palace of Holyroodhouse in Edinburgh. The trees bore huge and juicy crops and in one year of exceptional plenty the local policeman was deputed to guard the crop, which was in danger of being raided, no doubt by unemployed miners, who always got the blame for such thefts and for poaching the laird's policies.

So far as poaching was concerned, the miners certainly regarded this both as a hobby and, by reason of political conviction, a right. Our pits were for the most part small and the miners rural in outlook. No game could exist for long in the immediate vicinity of a pit and, in addition to this, the miners were passionate fishermen. They would fish from the rocks where the tide came right up to the back rows of the houses at Prestonpans, and a few even had little syndicates to run leaky old crab boats which sneaked along the coast setting their creels. This work was semi-clandestine, not because it was illegal to fish, but because every unemployed man lived in constant dread of snoopers, both unpaid and official, from the dreaded means test, who were constantly trying to find a way to cut the miserable allowances paid to those who had exhausted their "burroo" money and were trying to live off public relief.

133

Fortunately there are no riparian rights over brown trout in Scotland and, as our county sloped up to the Lammermoor hills, all the burns which came tumbling down to the sea were full of trout, to be taken on the worm or the wet fly and even by the odd purist using a dry fly. I even met an old miner once in later days, the days when pesticides had killed off that deadly bait for trout, the grub of the ghost moth, who showed me his unique substitute by which he swore. This unsung genius would buy half a pound of macaroni which he would lightly boil until it was "al dente". He would then paint two little black spots on the end of each piece and thus he had perfectly simulated ghost moth grubs complete with eyes.

So far as game was concerned, this was mainly rabbits, partridge and pheasant. Rabbits were commonly ferreted and this was a night-time occupation for a gang of three. When the burrows were stopped up so as to leave only an entry for the ferret and an exit for the rabbits, one man would work the ferret with a bag over the exit and the other two would watch "shot" for the keeper or the "polis".

Most poaching, in fact, was done at night. Pheasants would be taken with a slingshot while they could be spotted roosting on the pines by moonlight. Sometimes they could even be overcome with the fumes of a can of smouldering sulphur held on the end of a long pole. The bolder spirits would use a .410 shotgun for this work and rely on speed and, if necessary, aggression to let them get away. Partridges would roost in the middle of a favourite field at night and they could be taken with a net, provided that the keeper hadn't put bunches of whin in the field, or provided that these could be moved before the partridges had settled in for the night.

Hares were taken by coursing them with whippets, those mean, lean and shifty-eyed hounds which, along with the equally repellent greyhounds, so many miners loved to own.

To return to the plum orchards, it was a fine September evening when the policeman patrolling the plum trees was asked into the farmhouse for a cup of tea. The whole village laughed at the story of how he sat down at the kitchen table and, remarking what a hot night it was, took out his handkerchief to mop his brow, thus allowing a half-dozen of the very finest Victoria plums he had stuffed up his sleeve to roll onto the table in front of the farmer and his wife.

CHAPTER
SEVENTEEN

The Sea, the Whale and Fishing

The whole village and its surroundings were our playground, but above all we loved the sea. Ours was not especially a seaside village. Indeed, the high-water mark was about half a mile from the village centre, although some of the new "toffs'" houses were only a couple of hundred yards from the sand, separated from the shore by the road and the width of the golf-course which ran alongside. This golf-course served the very useful purpose of preventing the ribbon development of bungalows which despoiled so many seashores during the 1920s and '30s. For us it presented an ideal place, with its sandy hillocks, where we could roll our Easter eggs and during the winter we could slide with homemade sledges.

The older boys in the village and some of the young men from the little mining towns to the west, so many of whom were unemployed, would spend most of their summer days hanging about the caddies' room at the clubhouse in the hope of earning the odd sixpence or shilling carrying clubs. Of course there were the regular caddies, and some indeed like those who lodged from time to time with us, who actually could make a steady living from the game, particularly if they had a real knowledge of the course. Inevitably there was a card school at the caddies' room and, with equal inevitability, most of the lads went home as skint as they started out, while one or two sharp gamblers made more by playing cards than by carrying clubs.

Unemployed men scoured the bushes and the rough in the hope of finding the odd golfball which they could repaint and sell for three or four pence. This of course was illegal, and from time to time some miserable old man was hauled up to court and fined two and sixpence for "stealing a golfball by finding".

Two burns ran through the golf-course and there, safe beneath their banks and unseen, we could fish for minnows and sticklebacks. Here also we could, in all innocence, find the odd golfball and sell it for a penny to one of the searchers, who thus could buy at trade rates from us for resale at a hundred per cent profit. Not so innocently, but as often as we dared, we employed another stratagem.

One of the bunkers and a hole and driving green were situated across the road on the seaward side, and on the turf, just outside the perimeter of the bunker, we could safely and legitimately lie and sun ourselves. Every now and then a golf ball would lob over the edge of the bunker and, if the drive had been a long one, we could quickly crawl over unseen and bury the ball in the sand at the side. When the golfer came up he would commence his search and, after a couple of minutes, we would innocently ask if he needed help. Sure enough, one of us would "discover" the ball and sometimes, although not always, be rewarded with a penny. On a good day the pitch might be worth tuppence, but it was not wise to play the trick too often. It was also tiring work and there were so many rival attractions on the beach. We could play on the sand dunes and explore caves, in constant danger of inundation. The beach shelved only very gradually, so that we could walk quite a way out to sea before we needed to swim. We all swam, of course, although no one actually taught us to do so. For reasons which I shall detail later, I was never a strong swimmer and I did not dive at all, but all my sisters both swam and dived like champions.

Some boys did not swim and some indeed, those who had come to the village from big towns, would not even take their clothes off. One such youth was Ernie Larkin, whose father was English and whose mother came from Glasgow and was tiny, with a tiny voice. Mrs Larkin spoke in a soft, breathless whine and she went about the village borrowing things, partly from necessity and partly from sheer habit. Since she seldom gave back anything she had borrowed, she had to work on an ever-widening perimeter, only covering her old ground nearer home when her previous "tapping", if not forgotten, at least was no longer felt with strong resentment. "Do you think, Mrs McVeigh, that I could have a cup of sugar?" Mrs Larkin, who lived at the other end of the village, would whine, and mother would oblige. "Do you think, Mrs McVeigh, that you could give me just half a loaf until Friday?", and a day later: "If you have a couple of eggs . . ." — she knew mother had them, for she had seen me buy them at the village shop — "I would be ever so grateful — we have nothing at all in the house." Mother would add some potatoes, and this would go on until it could go no further. It was difficult to be rude to Mrs Larkin and she knew it, and this persistence was the basis of her technique. Her credit exhausted, Mrs Larkin always fell out with her supplier. She had, as she would always put it, "a little misunderstanding", and this left the door open for her to call back six months or a year afterwards, so that she could clear up the "misunderstanding" and start mooching once more.

All the Larkins were liars. In fact, they all lied in their teeth. They were all dirty as well, and the father had the old professional British soldier's ability to be at once dirty but smart in appearance. Our house was bare and battered, but as clean as mother could make it. The Larkins' house was dirty and smelled and, as I discovered once, had a pot full of nameless filth parked underneath the bed.

Ernie Larkin, then, came down to the sea but didn't take his clothes off. He had, however, the rare and unusual talent of being able to stand on his head in the shallow tide at the edge of the sea and at the same time to play "A hundred pipers an' a'" on the mouth organ. In what direction this talent, properly nurtured, might eventually have developed was never discovered for, at the age of 13, Ernie Larkin went to sea as a cabin-boy. I saw him some months later with a torch which he claimed to have bought in Hong Kong and which he was hoping to sell for two and sixpence. I discovered later that his ship sailed between Leith and Kirkcaldy.

While there was sand aplenty along our beach, there were even more rocks and rock pools. Rock pools have crabs and sea anemones and small fish and eels, and other nameless delights. We seldom wore shoes in the summertime and the soles of our feet were leather-hard. Even though the rocks were covered in barnacles, we could run and jump over them without thinking. This never occurred to me as anything remarkable until one day I noticed how painfully difficult it was for the children of some visitors to walk on the rocks. Even then I took it for granted that they must all have some obscure affliction of the feet and legs and dismissed the matter from my mind.

As we boys grew older, we took to fishing from the rocks and at times this became almost an obsession. Most of the fish were young saith or "podleys", as we called them, a species of no great culinary value and of quite outstanding stupidity. We caught them with the insides of mussels on a fairly coarse hook at the end of a sealine. None of us of course could afford a proper rod, so we made our own out of canes or willow wands. With a split cork as a float, we could catch fish while the tide was making and it was fairly calm. A dark sea was best, the kind that you get on an overcast day after rain. We would walk out to the farthest rocks just as the tide was turning and we would fish for hours, retreating along the rocks as the tide covered them. From time to time some lucky boy would catch a mullet or even a big eel, but it was mainly the saith, and these went to feed the village cats. The rocks could be lonely at times and very often we were reluctant to leave a good spot. When the tide would gradually force us off them, we would have to leap or wade to safety. Fortunately we could all swim and, in any event, for some reason which remains obscure to me, God likes boys and usually sees them return home wet but alive.

We even went down to the sea in winter. On the short Sunday days we would walk along the tideline. If it was calm we would throw flat stones along the water and watch them skim and bounce, or "stot" as we would say, along the surface, holding competitions as to whose stone could stot the greatest number of times before sinking. When the water was stormy, we could watch the great seas roll in and we could run along the tidelines, judging to the last second when we could leap out of the way before we were soaked by the broken wave.

The storms and the high tides of autumn and spring were exciting times for us. We would follow the tideline for flotsam, always in the hope that we would discover treasure. We never did, of course, but we did find all sorts of curious pieces of wood, some of which were very old and obviously had lain trapped under the sea for a very long time.

When father was alive he had gone down to the beach after the storms and carted back the baulks of timber he had found there. From these he had built our two chicken-houses, now neglected and empty, and two lean-to's at the back of the house. He had built them well, as with everything he did, except work for a boss.

When he was alive, I had loved to go down to the foot of the long garden and feed the hens with the hot bran mash, always taking a little for myself. I loved also to collect the eggs from beneath the softly clucking hens, holding the eggs in my hand and feeling their warmth, with the smell of feathers and the fine down getting up my nose and making me sneeze.

To get to the chicken run we had to go through the rose bower that my father had built from driftwood and old lathes, and with a swing in the middle for us to play on. The roses were pale pink and white and on a summer morning they smelled fresh and sweet, hanging heavy with dew.

The sea threw up other things after the storms: all sorts of marine life which normally belonged deep in the water or far out to sea. The odd dead shark or pilot whale was washed up, and one morning we could hardly believe our eyes when we saw a truly great whale which must have been over 30 feet long and about six or eight feet high. It already stank and it had a huge gash in its side, where perhaps it had been hit by the propeller of a steamer. We later watched fascinated, and upwind, as workmen from the "cooncil" cut it up into great sections with axes and crosscut saws and buried it in lime in a nearby quarry.

Once Kathleen, I think it was, came home in hysterics. She and friends had been walking on the shore when they saw a large bundle bobbing slowly in the water. It was a man with his face black and swollen, his body bruised from the rocks and his mouth full of sand.

CHAPTER
EIGHTEEN

The "Flapper" Track; Drownings at Sea

At the mining town about seven miles away from us there was a "flapper" track for racing greyhounds. This meant that both the track and at least some of the bookies who operated there were unlicensed, and with only the regulation of the pressures exerted by the miners who went there. It was a rough place and the bookie who failed to pay out had to take at least a beating and very often much worse. This bookie had got into debt by a series of bad races or the classical mug's game of backing his own fancies, to the tune of about 50 pounds. This was a vast sum which he knew he could never repay, and he just walked into the sea one night.

These "flapper" greyhound tracks continued to exist after the war, and indeed may do so yet. In the 1960s I was in charge of a small sales staff which included an ex-miner from Gorebridge. Bob was a nice man but he was not destined for success in life as a salesman, for he had a serious disposition and was utterly without humour. "Bob," I said to him once, "you take life too seriously. No customer likes to deal with someone with a long face." "A ken, Mr McVeigh," said Bob in his best Gorebridge English, "but it wisnae ay like it is the noo." When he was young, Bob explained, he had led what he described as a "dissipated youth". This meant that he drank a lot of beer, swore, and he raced and backed greyhounds at the flapper tracks. "A got intae an awfu' state," he said. "A owed the bookies 30 pounds and they were gaen tae gie me a hammerin' if a didnae piy. Ma ain dug wis runnin' in a race wi' twa ithers and a kent it wid win and a kent whit dug wid come second, sae a nobbled ma ain dug an' backed a' a could on the ither dug." "And how did you nobble your dog, Bob?" I asked. "Weel a'll tell ye: A fed it twa hot pies and wrapped an elastic band roon its ba's." "And the other dog won the race? "Naw," said Bob, "ma ain dug won, and that's hoo a'm sae serious the day."

Not long after the incident of the body in the sea there was another and greater tragedy when one of the best of the local fishing boats was driven ashore in a storm and her crew of four were all drowned. This was the *Budding Rose* of about 20 tons with a deckhouse and a good diesel engine and even a shortwave wireless, things which very few inshore boats had in those days. We walked along the beach in the morning to see her, broken and on her side with her deckhouse and masts gone. I climbed aboard her, but there was little to see. On a heap of ballast at the bottom of the boat I came across an old army greatcoat and took one of the buttons which I kept for many years.

The timber hunters and the seas soon took all but the ribs of the *Budding Rose* but today, almost 65 years later, I found her keel and a little bit of her stern embedded in the sand together with the stones from the ballast.

CHAPTER
NINETEEN

The Tallyman,
Rag Rugs and
the Drysalter

Most of the books in our house came from jumble sales, and at jumble sales it was always possible to get a whole bundle of books for a penny or even a halfpenny. There were, in fact, times at the end of a jumble when one got books for nothing, and we always hung about in this hope. Our reading therefore was, to say the least of it, catholic and by the age of eight I had tried my hand at, amongst others, Charles Dickens, Marie Stopes, Sir Walter Scott, Mrs Beeton and the anonymous author of *The Awful Confessions of Maria Monk*. We would, in fact, read anything except perhaps the Bible which mother read with deep conviction and sincerity every night but on which I was not too keen.

At this time — and it may well still be the case — there was a whole stable of weekly magazines published by D. C. Thomson in Dundee. Apart from the love tales and hinted scandal which Kathleen read so constantly, there were boys' magazines, such as the *Rover*, the *Wizard*, the *Adventure* and the *Hotspur*, all printed on cheap paper with two-colour illustrations on the cover. The contents were basically the same. The hero was a cowboy or an explorer or a gallant soldier who always triumphed at the end. No females intruded into this world but, curiously, with magazines published solely for a working-class readership, each magazine ran stories of a boys' public school and its heroes and its villains. We could not afford to buy any of these "magazines" regularly but they did have a residual value of a sort, in exchange for other copies of the same sort or even barter of various kinds.

My own favourite reading was sea stories or stories connected with the sea, and we were lucky indeed to have battered copies of books by R. L. Stevenson, R. M. Ballantyne and Captain Marryat. On winter nights I would read by candlelight in my bedroom. There were never enough blankets, but an old coat of father's helped to keep out the cold. I could see the light on the beacon of Inchkeith as it flashed with the revolving turret, or, on foggy nights, the broken note of its horn would boom through the mist. To read an adventure book in bed like that was sheer bliss for a boy, and I can think of no greater earthly delight.

I don't suppose that mother ever bought such wild luxuries as blankets and sheets in the years after father died. Certainly furniture of any sort or rugs and carpets were things we could never hope to acquire. To make a bedside cupboard, mother would cover an orange box with an old piece of curtain and use any balance to drape over the front. Working-class people even with

148

fathers alive and in jobs did not aspire to carpets in any case, or to rugs, at least if they were bought from shops. I played with one boy called Ian Dalziel, who lived in the same terrace but whose house was a vision of breathtaking luxury. I only went in there once and went, by some sort of mutual arrangement, no more. Ian's mother was houseproud and did not welcome scruffy little boys with muddy boots, and I for my part felt uncomfortable and tried to walk along the side of the room where the bare floorboards were, rather than over the highly polished linoleum. The house, besides, had a strong and rather strange smell which at the time I could not place. It took me several years and many houses later to realise that that particular smell came from the universal tool of all houseproud wives, "Mansion" wax polish.

All feet were muddy in those days and every house had a foot scraper beside the front door. The farm cottages in fact had an iron scraper fixed beside each door lintel, and above this, just at waist height, one could see a deep and smooth depression on the sandstone lintel edge. This was the place where generations of workers had leaned on fine summer evenings and smoked their pipes and sharpened their pocket knives which they used, amongst a hundred other tasks, to cut their rough black tobacco plugs. As to rugs, there was always one before the fireside, but this hearth rug was of shreds of rag knotted onto sackcloth with an awl and arranged in patterns.

Making rag rugs was an occasion which usually involved the whole family, and very often friends as well. The base of the rug was usually a barley sack, opened out and washed. For weeks, rags of various colours had been collected — woollen ones were best- and cut up into strips about an inch and a half wide and about six inches long. These strips were then stitched through the barley sack and knotted tightly, leaving both ends free to form the "pile". Patterns of all sorts and colours could be created most attractively if the supply of rags and the artistic abilities of the weaver were adequate.

By an irony of fate, such rag rugs as survive today are keenly sought after by collectors of "folk art". The poor people who made them longed to be able to afford even the cheapest and most rubbishy factory-made article and would gladly have made a rag rug in exchange.

Sometimes the house floor was bare; some of the farm cottages had earthen floors, and sometimes they were of board. Mothers always aspired to cover these with cheap wax cloth, which never lasted but was soon worn and tattered. Our kitchen fireplaces, like all the newer houses, had grates which were black with bright steelwork on the hobs and edges. The grates had to be kept bright with a repellent semi-liquid polish called "Zebo" which exuded a sickly sweet smell, and the steelwork was polished with a fine piece of emery paper. These twin purgatorial products left women with hands which were lined black and sandpaper- roughened fingers.

Our waxcloth, when it was bought, although needless to say the McVeighs never managed to purchase any, came from a travelling and horsedrawn drysalter's van which went round the villages and farms. It was hung with cheap pots and pans and the kind of tin flask that every schoolchild and farm-labourer carried, and there were rolls of cheap linoleum (no one thought of actually fitting it into a room) and waxcloth or "American cloth" table covers, the kind that gradually peeled to reveal the cheap cotton underneath.

The main product of the drysalter, however, was paraffin carried in a big tank and dispensed into cans with a funnel. Electricity had come to at least some of the houses in the village, although only for lighting purposes, but all the farm cottages were still lamplit. Paraffin was also universally used to repel the bugs which infested the older houses, and from the drysalter one could also buy a product called "Keating's Powder" which, if it didn't actually kill fleas, was said to make them sneeze so much they would go away and bother somebody else. Like every other family, we had to use this powder liberally. It came high on our list of priorities, together with a liquid which mother used in conjunction with a fine toothcomb to keep lice and nits down to an acceptable level.

Every night we would lean our heads over a newspaper while mother dipped the comb in a bowl and tugged away at the hair on our heads. If we saw a louse fall and start to run, we would quickly flatten it with our thumbnail, and then at the end of the procedure the newspaper would be shaken into the fire. Fleas were somewhat hardier. They could hide in corners in a room, for months it was said, until the chance of a meal came along. They could also leap enormous heights and it was almost impossible to crush them to death, at least between one's fingers. I admired fleas.

The drysalter's van smelled of tin plate, carbolic soap and paraffin and, somehow or other, of romance and plenitude.

New clothes had to be bought occasionally. The girls could get each other's hand-me-downs, and mother on trips to Edinburgh always managed to buy something in the secondhand shops for a few coppers which, if it did not fit one of the girls, would certainly fit an older or a younger sister. The girls quarrelled endlessly about clothes, as all sisters do, but this passed almost completely over my head for, if I wasn't out playing or working, I was completely immersed in a book. I would even read at the table, a bad habit it is true but one which mother allowed, perhaps in the hope that it would modify my appetite. This habit, I'm afraid, stayed with me until adult life, and when I went into the army I tried to continue it there, with results wholly unforeseen by me.

Some new clothes had to be bought then, particularly footwear, although — apart from a new pair of corsets mother wore the same widow's weeds all the years we were in the village after father died. These sartorial requirements were met by the travelling "shilling a week man" or the "tally" man, as we knew him. In Ireland he was known as the "Kathleen

152

Mavourneen man" after the method of payment: "It may be for years and it may be for ever."

The tallyman would call, parking his bicycle outside the front door but not removing his cycle clips. He contrived to wear a soft hat and always had a row of fountain pens in his outside pocket, which impressed me greatly. There would be a quiet consultation with mother, who always held a little notebook in her hand. The tallyman would take the book and write something in it, bid mother good-day and ride off on his bike. A few days later a new pair of shoes or trousers or a coat would arrive in the post. If it was trousers or shoes, I would be allowed to wear them to school and was strictly enjoined not to play with them on and to change them when I got home and before I had my tea. The hope was to keep a respectable appearance at least for Sunday, but it was a battle mother couldn't possibly win, and she knew it.

The tallyman had to be paid, of course, and this was the really hard part of the job for both him and mother. Few people paying off the tallyman were foolish enough to answer the door without peering around the edge of the window first. His whole life must have been dominated by stratagems to open doors and collect shillings before they were spent elsewhere or went to mark the books of rival tallymen, for the profession was a crowded one and many families had not one but three or four "on the tally", playing a weekly Russian roulette with their payment books. Mother couldn't always pay, but she faced up to her responsibilities. Sometimes indeed she "had to go out" but she always gave me a neatly written note "to hand to Mr Campbell when he comes". Sometimes there would be another little whispered consultation with Mr Campbell, this time without the book being marked, and he would give mother a little smile, pat her on the shoulder and ride off on his bicycle. Since mother always paid her debts, he really had little to worry about and I liked Mr Campbell. He once paid me thruppence to collect a great big basket of elderberries, "Bountry" berries as we usually called them, as his wife wanted to make some elderberry wine. I thought him both rich and rather simple, for there were so many elderberries in our woods and bawks that I could have got him a hundredweight for the same price.

When you are very poor, minor changes in the pattern of life which alter financial arrangements in even the slightest of ways can bring near-disaster to the fragile edifice of survival. Thus it was with mother when Mr Campbell departed to make way for a new tallyman who was large and young and brusque and who rode a motor bike. There was no more quiet understanding, no more stretching of credit, but a literal interpretation of the phrase "playing it by the book".

After the new tallyman's first visit, and after mother's usual quiet explanation, this time cut short, and his abrupt departure, mother sat down on the nearest chair. She took out her handkerchief (these were survivors of better times and were small with a lace edge and they smelled of the wild lavender she stored them with). "That's your pigeon," mother muttered. "How could he say that to me?" "That's your pigeon," she kept repeating over and over again. A sense of dignity is just as precious to the poor as it is to the rich. If the tallyman had run a knife through mother, he could not have wounded her more.

CHAPTER
TWENTY

Mother and the Dramatic Society

Mother was always sorry for people. "Think of all the poor children who are starving," she would say as she cut us a "piece" of bread and jam. When the wind blew hard she immediately worried about "all these poor men at sea", and when it rained she fretted for all the Indians trapped by the monsoon or the Chinese who had to flee the Yellow River. Mother even worried about the rich "who have all these responsibilities" and the Royal family "who must be completely tired out by all that pomp and ceremony". Once mother even played the part of Santa Claus at the annual school party and, inevitably, before delving into her bag for our sad little presents she felt compelled to remind us all that "many poor children" (God knows what she thought *we* were) "will get no presents at all at Christmas".

Father had voted Labour with passion and intensity. He didn't envy the rich, for father envied no-one, but he pitied the error of their ways. Mother had voted Labour when father was alive. She had compassion for everyone trapped by the human condition. Her politics, however, were slight and she thought, no doubt quite rightly, that if the whole world would just read the Bible and live by it, then the miseries of life would cease. Until that time she declared that there would "always be rich and poor" and that she thought she might vote Liberal next time but I fancy, for father's memory, she continued to vote Labour.

Mother was a born actress and she was always in demand for the one-act plays of the "kitchen comedy" type which were staged by the "Rural", the Women's Rural Institute, with suitable co-option of the necessary males. Mother on stage was transformed. She radiated a presence and an assurance which even today are remembered by those who saw her. She undoubtedly would have been a professional actress of the first rank, given other times and circumstances.

The "Rural" and the Dramatic Society were the sole outside enjoyments in mother's life. She would come home from the triumph of her performance on stage, get a basin of hot water and cut her corns which, as always, were "killing her". She would then go to bed and eat her little square of Fry's chocolate and, perhaps, half an orange.

That was my mother and that was her life. It is said that people are twisted and bitter because of circumstances, but how can this at least in every case be true? Alone in the world, and in insecurity and utter poverty, my mother brought up five young children and retained her sweetness and serenity of nature. That was the kind of person she was.

CHAPTER
TWENTY-ONE

Alan Lithgow;
Scarlet Fever

In the year of 1935, when I was between nine and ten years of age, my life was altered in two ways. This was the year of the Silver Jubilee of the reign of King George V and his queen. Looking at their pictures now in the style of clothes they wore, he an Edwardian gentleman and she with that high, stiff lace collar, they appear even more remote than they actually were.

We were given a holiday from school, and we paraded with the cubs and the scouts and the brownies and the guides and the Union Jacks which proclaimed that somehow we were superior to all the other nations of the earth. We had sports in the new playing field and we were all given a mug with a portrait of the king and queen on it, and there and then we filled it with tea and collected our bag of buns.

Shortly after this mother took me, washed and scrubbed, up to Edinburgh. This was a rare treat, the excursion to Woolworths, or a matinée performance of *Sanders of the River* at the cinema across the road from the Waverley Station. We went this time into a lawyer's office, which had a great brass plate by a massive painted door and an enquiry desk in the hall. I didn't know that this was an office, of course, still less a lawyer's office, but mother and I were taken into a room which was cold and smelled of the same polished smell as Ian Dalziel's house. Mother spoke quietly to a man and she told me to stay in the room while she went with him into a smaller room. My room was rather dark and it had some chairs and a settee, all of which were shiny and hard and covered in some material which had horse hairs sticking out of it in odd places, which scratched my legs and even poked through my trousers.

After some time the door of the other room opened and mother and the man were there with a boy who would be about the same age as me. "This is Alan Lithgow," mother said, "He is coming to live with us." I looked at the boy and he looked at me. He appeared to be quite a normal boy, with the usual number of hands and feet and dressed in normal clothes, although they were somehow a bit different from mine and there were more of them. He was a good bit larger than me, which again was normal, for although I was quick and strong, I was small for my age. The main difference from this boy, however, was his speech, which was like an Englishman's and at first quite difficult for me to understand.

The boarding-out of Alan Lithgow was yet another stratagem of mother's to keep our finances afloat. Alan was the child of a wealthy father, a well-known family in Scottish business, and a mother of whom little was known except that she had become so seriously mentally disturbed that she couldn't look after him. Mother was to get an allowance for his board, and the theory was that he was to be a companion to me.

Personally I had no particular wish for a companion, although Alan seemed quite a normal boy. I suppose I neither resented him nor took to him as a "brother". Certainly he was, for a time, an acquisition and I could show him off to my friends and even get him to speak for us in his funny English voice, which sent us all into great fits of laughter and attempts at mimicry.

We had to share the same room and bed, of course, and I didn't resent this either. Alan didn't have to work like me, however, and although we played together, there were other differences. The most important was that he was not in the slightest interested in reading while, to me, books were already my abiding passion in life. We went to school together and sat in the same class but, while all school work came without effort to me, to Alan school was the same purgatory, to be endured, which most boys found it.

Within a few weeks the upper-class English accent and speech were lost and Alan Lithgow was indistinguishable in appearance or speech from the other village boys. He was perhaps rather anxious to please my mother, and to get into her good graces by telling tales of misdeeds such as tree-climbing. But he was affectionate and amiable and we got on reasonably well, although soon Alan tended to play with his friends and I with mine. His background and arrival in

160

the village had not, however, been totally unnoticed, for on the birthday of the son of the home farm in the village, which was the largest and most important farm in the parish, Alan was invited, but not me.

Perhaps I can jump a little in time now and tell how, years after he left us, Alan Lithgow made contact with mother again. I was in the army at that time and serving abroad, and he was an apprentice electrician almost finished his time. I met him once when I came home, for he started to visit mother quite regularly. He was big and burly and still amiable, a typical decent working-class man with plans for marriage.

How relations with Alan Lithgow would have developed I don't know for, about three months after his arrival, I took ill and had to go to hospital. I had been ill only once before in my life and that had been before I was three years old. Then I had had a severe attack of bronchopneumonia. I don't remember much of this, but I know it was serious and that I had to be treated in the old-fashioned way with a steam kettle. This kettle still stood on a shelf in the outhouse, and I was left with a smaller than usual stature and rather an annoying cough but no other lasting effects.

Now, however, I had a high fever and I was sweating profusely and having nightmares, which I still remember, of great wheels which came rolling down at me. As fast as I jumped out of the path of one, another came at me, until I woke up shivering and soaked in sweat. So I was taken to the "fever hospital".

Although they weren't the killers which tuberculosis (or "consumption" as we always called it) in its various forms was, the twin diseases diphtheria and scarlet fever were common and, in their ways, could both cripple and kill.

> "When I had scarlet fever, they took me in a cab.
> The nurse she took my temperature and said I
>   wasn't bad.
> Then she grabbed a needle and unto me did come.
> Do you know where she stuck that needle, she
>   stuck it in my bum."

We sang this in hospital to keep our spirits up, and only children could be cheerful in circumstances such as these.

Local authorities had to build the isolation hospitals required by law, and in the hungry thirties both the buildings and the operation of the hospitals were as poor and as skimped as they possibly could be. The hospital was a mere collection of huts and the food was so dreadful that hungry as we were — and we were always ravenously hungry — some of it just could not be eaten.

The nurses must have been about as poor and certainly just as hungry as we were. No visitors were allowed, and the theory was that any food or fruit or chocolate or such-like gifts were to be handed in at the gate and shared equally among the patients. The nurses stole most of these edibles, and on special days each child would get a quarter of an apple or a small piece of chocolate or a couple of caramels. Even then we couldn't blame the nurses, who needed to steal our extras just to survive.

I cannot recall any medication, except that one initial injection and frequent doses of a fierce and liquid laxative, often given forcibly against screams, yells and curses of small boys who knew how to curse from their fathers. In consequence of this dosing, children frequently soiled the bed and, such was the sadism of some nurses, the rest of us were in continual terror of doing so.

Sometimes we would get a glimpse of parents or brothers or sisters out of the windows and across the grass, waving frantically to us over the high hedge which was the final barrier to the world outside. Norah and Mollie, cycling up from home, saw me in this way, and mother came once with Marion, by train. They had saved up to buy me sweets and fruit, of which I saw the usual minuscule portion, and mother, to whom it must have been the most colossal sacrifice, sent me a little note and a boys' paper, or small book of some sort, almost every day.

Many children got nothing, and there was no attempt at schooling or any distribution of reading material. It was in hospital that I started to read newspapers, a pernicious addiction which has stayed with me all my life. I would read some old magazine like the *Small Farmer's Gazette*, from cover to cover, including the advertisements and down to "printed and published by . . ."

The food varied very little. We were by no means fussy or discriminating in our eating habits but there was one dish, served several times each week, which few of us could stomach. This was tapioca pudding, which consisted mainly of large, glutinous lumps and was served without milk. For breakfast we had porridge and two slices of bread and margarine. This bread was of the kind that could easily be compressed into a solid lump of grey putty. We ate it, however, and we always looked around in the hope that some new patient was too ill or insufficiently hungry to eat his share.

For dinner (which the English called lunch) we had soup and the dreaded tapioca pudding or, on other days, mince and potatoes and semolina pudding. We were so hungry that we licked our plates, which were of enamelled iron with great sores where the enamel had chipped off. For tea we had bread and jam and tea to drink. Again the bread was strictly rationed and we never got anything extra. I cannot recall ever being given vegetables, either fresh or cooked, and this as much as the scarlet fever no doubt made the frequent purgatives so great a necessity.

The usual stay in hospital was five weeks, but I was fated to spend eleven weeks there. My left ear started to suppurate and my glands to swell and there was a mastoid condition which, it was thought, might necessitate removal to a legitimate hospital for an operation. This is what had happened to my sister Marion, who had survived but with a personality both larger than life and unstable. Fortunately it did not happen to me, but when eventually I was discharged my ear drum was perforated and continued to suppurate, sometimes painfully, for several years. This was the reason why my swimming henceforward was confined to a kind of side stroke which kept my "bad" ear out of the water, and why I never learned to dive.

I can remember little kindness in that hospital; we were never treated as worthwhile human beings, far less with the tolerance and patience that children deserve. One or two of the nurses were cruel, possibly with the cruelty of bitterness, but most of them were just people doing a job, with about the same enthusiasm or sense of vocation as women working in a biscuit factory.

It would be easy enough to condemn them, but now I know that mother's attitude to life had much more understanding than I then realised. We were all victims of the human condition, certainly in this instance. The nurses had to suffer more than we did, for they were fated to spend their days in that parody of a hospital while, apart from those of us who died (and death was not uncommon), we would soon be free to continue with the glorious adventure of childhood.

CHAPTER
TWENTY-TWO

The "Poison Pen" Letter; New Neighbours

It was already summer when I came home, and within a short time I discovered that in some way the scarlet fever had meant some sort of catharsis to my system, for I started to grow and develop very rapidly, a process that continued until I was twelve years of age and then abruptly stopped.

I made the dreadful discovery, seeing mother's distress, that some poisonous-minded person in the village had sent a letter to Alan Lithgow's guardians alleging that he was being ill-treated by mother and half starved. The lawyers did not allow mother to see the letter, but only to know the gist of the allegations. They sent an emissary to question Alan, and their concern was all for him and not for the distress caused to mother by what was obviously a series of shoddy little lies. I realised that mother almost certainly knew who had written the letter, but she was never able to expose the culprit, and I doubt if she would have wished to.

The grieve on the home farm had been a friend of father's, and when mother was widowed he would occasionally help her by planting some potatoes in the garden. He was a good and simple man who had married a little above his station in life, or so his wife thought. She was English, and she had been a lady's maid in the "big hoose" before she married. She had picked up phrases from her employers which, she was convinced, gave her a refined accent. I recall that she called me "a dear little boy", which made me acutely embarrassed as I knew I was not "dear" and resented the reminder that I was little. She powdered her face heavily, at a time when no village working-class women wore any cosmetics, and she did no other work than looking after her house, taking a walk along the village every afternoon. Once more this was a strange habit, and one which she no doubt considered ladylike, for no working-class women normally walked anywhere unless there was a distinct purpose in doing so.

The couple had one child, a boy called Billy, who was older than me and had been crippled suddenly by poliomyelitis. He was destined to die at the age of fourteen. I liked Billie and I liked his father, who made me a "guider", a splendid barrow with real pram wheels, that I could steer and that had my initials painted on the side. I didn't like the mother, who ingratiated herself with my mother and took cups of tea with her, breaking the routine of her afternoon walk to do so.

I am sure this dreadful woman regarded mother with a mixture of admiration that here was a real lady, envy that she had so many children, and bright children at that, and not a little real hate. From mother she would

167

have prised out the details of Alan's lawyer guardians piece by piece over her almost daily afternoon cups of tea. It may even have been that she nurtured murky ideas about her innocent and amiable husband who had helped mother but, in any event, here almost certainly was the author of the squalid letter which had caused mother so much grief.

They are both long dead now, the perpetrator and the innocent victim, but time has left a feeling of great sadness that the poor could still on occasion afford feelings of such malice, to add to the burden of their poverty.

It was not long after that when Alan Lithgow left us. Mother's innocence had been established, but things were never the same and, in any event, payment from the lawyers had often been irregular, which had almost cancelled out any economic advantage to mother in the arrangement. I felt no sorrow at Alan's going, and I feel none now. I do perhaps harbour a little guilt that we never became real friends, but that was the way it was. Years after when he started to visit mother, I suppose he felt lonely and longed for the home life he never had. Perhaps when he married he really had a home for the first time. In any event we saw him no more.

Our neighbour through the wall, who cried so loudly and so long each time her husband had to be taken away to the mental asylum, finally left us. In the place of the poor man, his wife and their children, we got neighbours of a very different kind.

The Browns, inevitably known in the Scots way as the Broons, consisted of the father, Sandy, and the son, also Sandy, with the mother, Lizzie, and the daughters Lizzie and Lindy. As a family and as individuals they were rough, noisy and slatternly. They were, in fact, "coorse" in every way, and Sandy senior was as coorse as his wife, which was saying quite a lot. Sandy worked on the railway, for he had done so before the war and, although he was — like all the menfolk in our street — badly wounded, he had been taken back by the railway company and given a light job in the parcels office. Besides the station-master who collected the tickets, our station supported Sandy in the parcels bothy, in which a great fire burned all the year round, and the porter Mr Mackay.

Sandy chewed tobacco, spat and cursed. He also stole eggs from the wicker baskets simply by sliding his hand under the lids. He would snatch an egg and crush it in his hand with the palm uppermost and then, withdrawing his hand, he would lick the yolk off his palm and fingers and wipe them on the leg of his trousers.

Mr Mackay was an amateur historian and a militant Scottish Nationalist, then a very rare breed indeed. He would question Norah, who every afternoon waited for the newspaper train: "Whit are ye gettin' at the skule the noo, lassie?", he would ask. Norah would innocently tell him about Wolfe in Canada or the Indian Mutiny. "Can they no' tell ye aboot the history o' yer ain country?" Mr Mackay would mutter. Then,

169

as the paper train showed along the track and the noise of its arrival grew louder, the mutter would gradually become a shout: "Dinna trust thae English", Mr Mackay would bellow, "an dinna trust thae Hanoverians as weel."

Mrs Broon was large, with red arms and with wispy grey hair pinned perilously above her head. She always wore a large sack as an apron and she always exuded damp and the smell of soapy water. Despite the fact that she appeared to be constantly busy, her house was a midden; she was a "slaister" in fact. Her voice was as powerful as her man's. "Saundy," she yelled one day, and we all heard her through the wall after Sandy had decided to take an eventual bath: "Saundy, this bath's a' glaur [dirt]."

Illness, possibly some form of bone tuberculosis, had left Sandy junior with a deformed rib-cage. He was about twelve years of age when he came to live next door to us. He was cheerful and good-natured and never seemed to mind his mother's constant references to his condition, which she proclaimed to all who would listen. "Puir Saundy," his mother would announce like a foghorn: "Puir Saundy, he's goat a doo's kist [pigeon chest], ye ken, he'll no live long," and she would nod in vigorous agreement with herself. The older of the two girls, Lizzie, who was about 17, was a frequent visitor to a tent in the back garden, where the Broons' lodgers were accommodated. These were two youths who in the summer earned a precarious living as golf caddies and who slept in the

170

tent, having their supper in the house. One evening Lizzie emerged rapidly from the tent in a more than usually dishevelled state, announcing loudly that she was "no playin'". What game Lizzie had refused to play I never knew, but I did find out that Lindy (who was learning the banjo) was a child old beyond her ten years or so.

One day Lindy approached me in a conspiratorial way. I was about eight years old at the time. "Come roon' the back o' the hoose," she commanded. I meekly went and she pushed me into the door of the shed. "Gie's a ride," she requested, and she lifted her none too clean dress high above her waist to reveal that she was knickerless. Lindy was nothing if not direct, and I have from an early age been an obliging soul, but I didn't know what she meant, and indeed I question if she had more than a vague idea herself.

Like all children we had had a vague curiosity from time to time about the differences in the anatomy of boys and girls. This was usually satisfied in a group way with a bolder boy or girl displaying themselves briefly while the rest of us fell about laughing and threatening to "clipe" (tell) on the brazen hussy or the "gallus" (bold) boy.

Lindy repeated her urgent request and, to emphasise it, she opened my trousers and grabbed my small penis, unfortunately squeezing my equally small testicles in the process. I let out a yell of pure agony and Lindy departed swiftly, before any adult might come on the scene. That, for some years, was the extent of my sexual experience, but for Lindy I expect

171

it was only the beginning. There were plenty of big boys on the farms, already lecherous and knowing all there was to know, and our village had no shortage of secret places.

The sister Lizzie eventually fell in love, or at least the man who courted her loved Lizzie. He was a shepherd who lived in one of the farm cottages in the village with his idiot sister. He was a good and kind man, a "canny man" as we would say, and he looked after his sister with love and devotion. She could literally do nothing for herself, and on sunny days he would sit her outside the house before he cycled off to work with his two dogs running behind the bike.

All day the poor girl would sit crooning to herself, with a trickle of saliva running down one side of her mouth. She was totally unable to talk and very much alone, although a few kind people would stop in passing and give her a few words, while the girl grunted and nodded her head and tried to smile.

In the evening, the herd would feed his sister and put her to bed and somehow, even during the lambing season when he had to stay by the flock, he managed to look after her — feed her, wash her and comb her hair. Then the herd started to court Lizzie. Most of their courting took place in the bothy (hut) at the corner of the field used during the lambing. Soon it was evident that Lizzie was pregnant, "bairnt" as we always called it. The herd could not discard his sister and Lizzie would not or could not share the burden of looking after her, which would have been her lot if they had married. Thus Lizzie's first bastard child was born into a house like the Broons'. They had no front of respectability to lose, and they didn't give a damn anyway.

Despite everything, we live in happier times. No great stigma is now attached to the innocent child born out of wedlock, but in my day it was only the poorest and the most ignorant who — by the paradox of life — were usually able to give a fatherless child love and affection despite the scorn of the world.

Lizzie's courting, after an interval, was resumed and before I left the village she had given birth yet again. Of the eventual fate of this tortured romance I do not know. Perhaps I have passed a middle-aged man or woman in the street, respectable, with a house on a mortgage, with a motorcar, with carpets on the floor and a colour television set, who was conceived in that tumbledown bothy amongst the sheep in a corner of a lonely field so many years ago.

CHAPTER
TWENTY-THREE

Food

"Sex" may be only a vaguely understood word to a child, but food is a very different matter. I cannot say that food obsessed me in the same way that, for instance, reading a book or fishing obsessed me but at the same time, apart from the vile tapioca pudding and some of the dishwater soup in the fever hospital, I cannot ever remember refusing to eat, or indeed not being eager to eat whatever I had the good fortune to be offered. Porridge and brose still formed a goodly part of the farmworkers' diet and this was nourishing, filling and also cheap. For the single men housed in the farm bothies it was often almost the only food, supplied as it was by the farmer's wife as a part of the wages along with some skimmed milk.

The bothy lads, however, always seemed to be able to steal enough eggs from around the farmyard to provide a useful supplement. These were usually hard-boiled in the big kettle in which they made their tea. Pheasant eggs were filched as well and wild duck eggs could always be found in the springtime. These were always tested in the water nearby. If they floated, they were on the way to hatching; if they sank, they could be eaten.

174

Mother had come from a comparatively well-to-do background, and her father had in fact been in the fruit and vegetable trade. The Scots, however, like the Irish, could never remotely be classed as gourmets. Even now the working-class Scot eschews fresh fruit and vegetables and, given the choice, he will eat tinned peas even if he grows peas fresh on a farm.

In my day we were far worse in this respect, for we lived for the most part on a diet arranged through poverty out of ignorance. The land about our village is some of the most fertile in Britain and the sea nearhand abounds in fish. In many of the homes, however, sweetened tinned milk was actually preferred to fresh and one could always find a tin of this vile concoction on the table, while the great treat for Sunday tea was Canadian tinned salmon on white bread.

The same poverty of course compelled many people to eat at least some of their diet, for the most part the least regarded, in good wholesome food. But cheap cakes and white bought bread would always be eaten in preference to fresh potatoes or eggs or fresh milk. Most people, however, grew their own potatoes and a very high percentage kept hens, which they relied on to see them through the week.

Fresh vegetables, especially raw, were strangers to most tables. Even mother, with her background, never made a salad, although she was fond of tomatoes, which she would cut up and spread on bread. Mother would rather eat dry bread than bread and margarine, which she abhorred, but most of our vegetables were eaten in the form of soup.

Soup was the great filler, and for many of the households having only an open fire and an iron pot over a swee (a hinged bracket), it was the most convenient form of cookery next to boiled potatoes. Scotch broth was the universal soup and it was quite a treat to save the peas from this broth and take them to school as a supplement to the usual bread and jam. Potato soup, not unnaturally, came a close second and this was well flavoured with pepper. Mother was more adventurous and made lentil soup when a ham bone was available from the grocer.

Most meat was eaten in the form of mince, for this was the cheapest, but mince made slowly in an iron pan with onions was delicious. Also made in an iron pan were "stovies", best made with roast-beef dripping, some onions and turnip and plenty of pepper and salt. This was a filling dish and cheap, and whole families were brought up on Scotch broth and stovies, with white bread and jam eaten at midday in the fields or at school. Mother was a baker of near genius who, when she could afford it, and when our temperamental oven in the black range was working, could make wonderful cakes. In most houses without an oven, scones and bannocks could sometimes be made on an iron griddle hanging from the swee. It must be remembered, however, that on the farms most women worked in the fields or the byres, at least for the greater part of the day, and there was little time for real cooking even if the facilities had existed.

We had apple trees in our garden and for some reason, probably because he did not like to eat apples raw, father had planted only cookers. Being the essentially practical Irish peasant that he was, he combined his orchard with a hen run. Thus the hen dung had fertilised the apple trees and thus the hens had been partially fed by the windfalls. A garden like this looks and smells as a garden should. There is nothing in this world like the smell of a working garden on a summer morning. It is the compound of hens and roses and ripening apples and sweet grass, held ready by the night's dew and released gently as the sun rises and grows stronger.

The apple trees went unpruned after father died and the hens gradually died, but there were still apples aplenty for mother to cook and stew. Her main problem, in fact, was finding enough money for the sugar, but we delighted in stewed apples with their tangy taste and perhaps a little sweet rice in the dish. Mother also made jelly with apples and brambles, and this we ate in vast quantities while the farm children for the most part ate cheap and rubbishy jam, although the hedges around them were laden with brambles and even wild apples and "geens", the bright and bitter little cherries which grew along the south-facing woods.

Fish were cheap, of course, and little regarded. We ate mainly haddock, which mother fried in breadcrumbs. Fresh haddock is the king of all fish, and hake or salmon is as nothing beside it. Still, the tin of cheap Canadian salmon was regarded as the height of affluence and the greatest of treats.

We could have got fresh mussels from the rocks, and we did eat the buckies down at the beach, boiling them over a fire in an old tin and using a blackthorn as a pin. No-one, however, would think of taking these home as a dish. There were crabs, too, to be got from the far rocks at low tide, "partans", which only one or two people in the village would eat. There were crab and lobster boats working out of all the little harbours around us, but their catch was sent away to England and even to France, where people ate that sort of rubbish. Meanwhile our village grocer sold little jars of crab and lobster paste, which on special occasions was spread thinly on white bread.

CHAPTER
TWENTY-FOUR

Father's Relations;
The Burns Family

Father had relatives in Ireland but, with the element of mystery in his background, we saw or heard little of them. He did have a sister who had "gone wrong" by frequenting dance halls, but of her we knew little else. He also had a sister who had gone off, first to Toronto in Canada, where in fact so many Ulster folk go, and who had later moved down to Miami for the sake of her health, as she was asthmatic.

This sister, Lillian, came across on a visit when father was still alive, but I was too young to remember her at that particular time. She and mother did not get on too well, which is strange, or at least I always thought it strange until, many years later, I met her when she came to Scotland once more. Lillian had worked in hotels all her life, and there she met her husband Joe, who I suspect was quite illiterate. Joe was English and, like Lillian, an emigrant. He used to send us photographs of himself in his back garden in Miami, bared to the waist and tough and sinewy like a second Popeye the Sailorman. Joe was actually about five feet tall and his wife was even smaller. Lillian could only have stood about four feet nine in her shoes. She was representative of a particular physical type still common in Ulster, who can only be described as miniature people. I was surprised during my service abroad to find the same tiny people in the highlands of Apulia and Calabria, with the difference that these Italians usually were almost as broad as they were high, while the Ulster people were tiny in proportion.

Lillian and Joe, her husband, had gone to Miami about 1920, when it was largely still inhabited by snakes, alligators and a few Seminole Indians. They had bought land and built a house and the city had sprung up around them. Thus in the 1960s the Briggs house, a wooden bungalow set in its own large garden with a stream, amongst the concrete of central Miami was one of the most valuable pieces of real estate waiting to come on the market.

Lillian, however, was in no hurry to die, and neither was Joe. She came over to see me in the 1960s, when she was in her mid-eighties, and at last I realized why she did not get on with mother and why, despite her asthma, she had lived so long. Lillian was charming and as tough as an old boot, and she gently but doggedly got her own way in everything she wanted or did. She was completely and charmingly and utterly a selfish wee devil, who bossed around everyone with whom she came in contact. I loved her, but at a distance.

We did have two Irish cousins who came over from Derry on holiday. These were boys of 16 or 17 or so, called Billy and Jim. They were charming and witty, and what Irishman is not, and they had their eyes on Kathleen, who was at home between jobs at the time. No doubt Kathleen with her silly notions encouraged them both, up to a point at least, but one day at the beach they took down her knickers, stuffed them with nettles and then put them back on again. Mother said nothing to me except that the two Irish cousins "had to go home", but nothing like this was ever very secret in our village for long.

We had another Irishman in the village, but he was of a different class. He was a retired naval captain and he lived in a house alone. He was a bachelor, with a maid-cum-cook who came in every day from the village. His house was down near the sea and stood apart, just where the path commenced across the golf course and down to the beach. He was extremely patriotic, British patriotic that is, and at every excuse he ran up a message in coded flags on the flagpole in his garden, congratulating the Royal Family on one thing or another. He was also extremely sharp- tempered and irascible, so it was perhaps a mistake that his nephew from Ireland, a youth in his late teens, came for an intended visit of several months. Unfortunately the lad was addicted to practical jokes and his uncle quickly came to the end of his tether.

At length the captain threatened that the next stupid joke his nephew perpetrated, off he would go back home to Ireland. It was not long after that, on a cold and dark night while the captain was sitting by the fire and the cook was in the kitchen making the evening meal, that the door bell rang. The captain called through to the cook that he would answer the door, and this he did to reveal a small figure wrapped up in a greatcoat and scarf and with a hat pulled down over his eyes.

"Good evening," said the figure, "I'm the new assistant minister and . . ." "Oh", shouted the captain, "so you're the assistant minister. Well, meet the queen of Sheba. I'll give you assistant minister," he continued, and he pulled the figure into the hall and rammed his hat down over his ears and proceeded to punch him heartily in the ribs. "Back to Ireland you go," he yelled. "I've had enough of your silly jokes."

The captain's thumping ceased when he saw his nephew coming downstairs from his bedroom, where he had been all the evening, and the figure in the hall really was the new assistant minister. The cook, the nephew and the new assistant minister were all sworn to silence by the captain, but it was too good a joke to miss, and either the cook or the nephew let the cat out of the bag within a couple of weeks. The nephew went back to Ireland, and for months the flagpole in the captain's garden stood bare of flags.

We had other relations, of a sort at least, who during the summer were not very far from us. About four miles away along the coast was what for want of a better description was called a holiday camp. In the days before planning permission, during the 1920s and 1930s, it was common for people to build huts or to park caravans on any odd piece of land, either free or for a small ground rent. Such sites appeared to be quite haphazard, as were the type and standard of the habitations which occupied them. At the back of a railway cutting in our village there were several old railway coaches and one old tramcar sitting in the long grass, with only a stream nearby for water. In an old and abandoned lime quarry where we used to go to gather brambles and pick great bunches of gowans (what the English call "marguerites") there were many more huts and caravans and old bus bodies and even tents, and here there was only a little spring trickling down from the rock face to provide a source of water.

Such holiday homes were often given names like "Blue Heaven" or "Mon Repos", and the better of them even had a little fence with a garden gate at the front.

It was on such a site which, since it was in an open field by the sea, was steadily growing, that my "uncle" John Burns built a hut. He was not really my uncle and his wife Ella was not my aunt, but only a relative of my mother's by law. What sort of relative she was, or how far removed, I never found out. There is a declining species in Scotland consisting of middle-aged to elderly ladies, who could reel off the genealogy of their families and of all the families they knew. "Oh aye, Andra, him wi' the rid heid. That wis the wife's brither's guid cusin on his faither's side."

So we called the Burnses uncle and auntie and their children our cousins. Being on mother's side of the family, they were in the Plymouth Brethren but not, I think, in a very active way. Certainly their children, when they were in Edinburgh, went to the Brethren meeting house on Sundays, as indeed also did the McVeighs if they were trapped at their grandparents' over the weekend.

The Brethren meeting house — one could never call it a church — was the old schoolhouse, a tiny late eighteenth-century building in the Morningside district of the city. This was the district my grandparents inhabited, and indeed it was a stronghold of that unlovely creed. Morningside is a district inhabited, now as then, by the lower and aspirant middle classes, and it has always had a well-deserved reputation for snobbery. Like most minorities who stick close together and do not indulge in either the failings or the sociable habits of the crowd, the Brethren, most of whom came from fisherfolk stock, did well in small businesses of one sort or another.

The Burns family, and of course the McVeighs, were about the only exception in the congregation, and as decently but poorly dressed working-class children we felt this acutely. All the women, as I have already said, were over-dressed, with fur coats or at least those fox-fur collars with complete heads and staring eyes. The men had nap overcoats and homburg hats, and older men like my grandfather still wore top hats, while the older women tended to wear long velvet coats with fur trimmings and large hats with a veil. The children too were over-dressed, and many of the boys had kilt outfits. When we went to live in Edinburgh, I was sent regularly on a Sunday to this horrid place, and I felt alone and isolated in my threadbare short trousers amongst all these over-dressed and overfed people.

The Burns family were like us and therefore we felt a sort of solidarity with them. Uncle John worked in the fruit trade as a clerk. Although a working-class man, he had a good job, but his wage had to bring up a family of either nine or ten children. I forget the exact number, and sometimes I feel that Uncle John and Auntie Ella were not too sure themselves. One child had died as an infant, but the rest were healthy and hardy enough. I have a photograph of them all standing outside the hut, which Uncle John had built with his own hands. They are arranged in order of age and look exactly like a set of stairs in profile. There were about equal numbers of Burns children, male and female, and whatever sex they were and no matter what their age or size, they looked exactly the same. In my photograph the identity is made even closer by the fact that the Burns children are all clad in home-knitted garments. The small boys, and even the big boys, have knitted jerseys and short knitted trousers, and all but one of the girls wear knitted dresses. The oldest, a girl well into her teens, has a skirt and a knitted jumper.

All the Burns children had the same cheerful round face and gentle expression, and all of them loved their parents and loved each other. They spent the entire summer holidays at their hut, and I loved them and I loved their parents too. According to modern theory there should have been a snag in this somewhere, for the Burns parents were extremely strict. Uncle John was small and thin and quiet and strict. Auntie Ella was small and strict and almost unbelievably fat. She often sat in a chair, but it was difficult to tell if she was standing up or sitting down. She carried a walking stick with her everywhere, and she did not hesitate to use it freely on any of the children as they passed her, and the children adored her.

Father took me to visit the Burnses first of all. It was a four-mile walk along the shore and through the woods, and I'm sure he must have carried me at least part of the distance, because I was three years old. After father died and when I got old enough, I would walk to see the Burns family by myself. The way, or at least the short cut to the way, led through a long wood which we called the Baker's Wood because a baker was supposed to have hanged himself from a tree there. I once saw a magpie flying into the top of a dead tree at the edge of the Baker's Wood, and I climbed up to the top to have a look. Sure enough it was the magpie's hiding place for all his treasures — bits of rag and silver paper and bright shards of broken glass. What do magpies do nowadays, I wonder, when there is so much more brightly coloured litter lying around to choose from? Do they still hide things, or are they fed up with all the bright baubles they can pick up so easily?

We had all read of the magpie who steals the diamond necklace, of course, and I staked out my discovery, checking it several times a week in the hope that at least I would find a valuable ring there eventually. I let Mollie in on the secret and she climbed the tree to have a look. As she was coming down, a rotten old branch she was standing on broke, and she fell, scraping her back on the top of the dyke which ran along the wood's edge. I thought her back must be broken, but God was good to us that day, and Mollie was only scratched and bruised.

The Burns children ate vast quantities of home-made lemon curd on white bread. I'm sure they must have eaten other things as well, and they were all well nourished and healthy. Uncle John was in the fruit and vegetable trade, of course, and that was a godsend, particularly for potatoes and turnips, but it is the lemon curd I remember. All the Burns boys and girls married and became decent hard-working, well balanced husbands and wives. If there is a recipe for a straightforward, uncomplicated family life, the Burns family, all eleven of them — or was it the straight dozen? — had found it.

CHAPTER
TWENTY-FIVE

Grandfather's House;
My Uncles

Grandfather and grandmother still lived in the family house in which mother was born. This was a big house, at least by our standards. Downstairs there was a dining room with a huge side-board and a dining table and a red and green carpet and walls with paintings of mournful cattle in Highland glens. The entrance had a case of stuffed humming birds and the hallway had another green and red carpet. There was a study downstairs and then a long pantry and a kitchen with a scullery, and at the end of that a water closet which was intended for the maid's use. At the back there was a not very large walled garden which I found dull and without interest, unlike our large wilderness of a garden at home. Upstairs there was a bathroom and other rooms, and above that there were still more rooms.

This house was sliding steadily into decay, just as grandfather's fortunes were doing. Grandfather had two supreme disadvantages in life. The first of these was that he was a man of complete integrity and trust in business, so that he was owed a great deal of money by various people and had been fleeced of the rest by dishonest employees. His second disadvantage was that he had sired three boys, all of whom were cheats and crooks.

All of the boys had married and two of these resulting couples now lived in the upper stories of the parental home. Grandfather had been a director of a wholesale fruit and vegetable business and he had owned various retail shops in Edinburgh. He was now reduced to the status of an employee, and an increasingly minor one at that, and the two "boys" who had remained in the house had taken over the last two of the retail shops.

The eldest son, John, had a kind of ruthless charm and a sense of humour. He also had a taste for violence, perhaps aroused by his war service and perhaps also in part due to the fact that he had been hit on the head by the edge of an aircraft propeller blade and, as a result, had a steel plate in his skull. He had left the Air Force at the end of the war and, like so many other ex-officer drifters, he had joined the dreaded British Auxiliary Cadets during the Irish troubles. The "Black and Tans" had been bad enough, but it was the utterly ruthless "Auxies" who really had been given a licence to loot and murder. At the end of the Irish troubles Uncle John had come home to work with grandfather, but he still kept a cosh in a cupboard, and during the minor but bitter and periodic Orange v. Catholic disturbances of the 1930s in Scotland, he used this cosh with enthusiasm. Uncle John had always secretly drunk and womanised and bet on the horses. He loathed his brother Jim, who was the youngest of the three, and in return Jim cordially hated him. Jim had inherited the good looks and the sneaky disposition of Granny and eventually he was to inveigle himself into control of what was left of the family business. He was fly, but not fly enough, for although he had become engaged to a local middle-class girl who would help his finances on getting married, he fell victim to the charms of the well-upholstered Highland shopgirl in Grandfather's shop. Jim had paid dear for his moment of passion, for the girl had ensured that he had put her in the family way, and he had to marry her.

On her marriage, Jim's wife had brought several of her relatives down from the glen to Edinburgh, and Jim had to subsidise these as well as try to find jobs for them. Meantime his wife grew fat and ate chocolates and read "fast" books. I know, because I saw all of these things, including a book which was called *I Lost my Girlish Laughter*. I liked Jim's wife, and she was kind to me, and she had met that awful family on their own terms and emerged triumphant. I was to become more familiar with that horrid house shortly, but mercifully — although I went to live there — it was not to be for long.

Grandfather had been a jolly man, at least to us when we were children. He liked to laugh and he would say to Mollie: "Mollie the coo's name." He would get a thimble and place it on my cheek and then suck the air from it so that it stuck there. I could feel the prickles from his white beard as he did this, and he laughed all the while, but never with his eyes. He was a handsome man and a bit of a snappy dresser, with spats and a grey homburg, and a top hat on Sundays. I suspect that he had been a strict and even tyrannical father, but he was also capable of great kindness. I know this, for in later life I met several people who had come in contact with him and told me of his kindness.

At the start of the war, when I was working for the Forestry Commission cutting down trees and living in bothies and huts, I met a man who had been one of grandfather's clerks. George MacDonald was a conscientious objector who had been directed to forestry work. George was a pacifist by conviction, which was strange, for he was aggressive by temperament. He was deeply Christian, but before his conversion he had been on the wilder fringe of the Socialist movement. He wore a white stiff collar all the time, even working in the mud and dirt of the woods. He had flaming red hair and wild eyes and he still called everyone "comrade". George MacDonald had made his own cross in life, but he always spoke of my grandfather with respect and even with love, as a man of both principle and compassion.

Later on, when I came out of the Army and started to work as a navvy on a building site, I met a man who had sold fruit from a barrow on Saturday nights at the old market which once was held on the North Bridge of Edinburgh. He told me how many times grandfather had "subbed" him with enough stock to trade, or ensured that he got a good deal on a Saturday when the wholesalers had to get rid of the fruit which would not keep over the weekend. Now he was labouring alongside me and he claimed that it was grandfather who had finally got him to lay off the booze which was killing him.

Mother's third brother, Ian, was down in England, but he appeared from time to time in Edinburgh, or even at our village. He was egotistical and handsome, and I suspect that he had used his charm to such effect that grandfather at one time had set him up in business on condition that he lived as far away as possible. He had, in fact, a succession of businesses, all of which failed but from all of which he seemed to emerge, bankrupt but still able to run a car, that rarest of luxuries in the years between the wars. Ian's wife was English, and a lovely and loving person, who no doubt loved him, but was far too good for him.

All the brothers lived long lives and none of them gave a damn for mother in her distress and poverty. Mother grieved continually at their hatred of each other and she made excuses for their neglect: "Business is so bad; they have so many worries."

As grandmother and grandfather failed in health, their house was mortgaged and grew scruffy. The maid went, and then the daily woman, and then Uncle Jim succeeded in ousting Uncle John from both the business and the house. Jim prospered, to an extent at least, and for the first time he started to interest himself in the McVeigh family but his interest, as always, was utterly devoid of any element of altruism.

What Uncle Jim was looking for was cheap labour, and the McVeigh sisters were just right for this. More than this, the McVeighs were honest and he knew they would never "skin" from the till or the stock. Uncle Jim had a manageress in the fruit shop who was the same age as mother, but who dyed her hair black and rouged her cheeks. Aggie had been inherited from grandfather's time and, whether it was because of this or because she had some sort of a hold on Jim, he could not or would not sack her. It was not so much that Aggie was addicted to stealing money: apart from her supply of cigarettes, it is unlikely that she opened the till for other than honest reasons. It was simply that Aggie, who was a spinster, did not use money when she went to buy anything she needed, whether it was a pair of stockings, an electric light bulb or a joint of meat. Aggie paid for almost all of her needs with Jim's fruit and vegetables, and she had done so for the twenty-five years she had worked in the shop.

The McVeighs, then, who would not even steal an apple from the box and who could be trusted, at least until they learned some sense, to work hard for low wages, were a potential godsend to Uncle Jim. More profound plans, however, were slowly being hatched in his unsavoury brain, and the implementation of those plans would eventually mean our leaving our village for ever.

CHAPTER
TWENTY-SIX

We Leave Longniddry

I was now almost eleven years of age. Mussolini had invaded Abyssinia and the bitter civil war in Spain was just commencing. I was old enough in the ways of the world now to go up to Edinburgh on mother's behalf, with neatly written notes, or sometimes a little packet, to the pawnshop. I still could go by bus or train, paying half fare, which was a certain saving in mother's desperate financial situation. Once or twice I even went as far as Morningside, to Uncle Jim's shop or grandfather's house.

The big city was still an exotic place for me, and a ride on the top deck of one of the old-fashioned open tram cars with its wooden benches was an enthralling experience. One of Uncle Jim's shops sold flowers and plants only and the other sold fruit and vegetables only. Grandfather had been brought up to the trade in the old-fashioned way and he didn't mix the two. He wouldn't even sell confectionery, and the greatest concession he made in this direction was to sell round boxes of crystallised fruits for the Christmas trade.

This was the busy time, as I was to discover soon. Uncle Jim had a nursery with hothouses where he brought on plants for the Christmas rush and at this time he sold things such as ornamental dried grasses with coloured chili pods wired on to them. These pods arrived in shallow boxes with wrappings from Spanish newspapers inside, and I would take these away and try to decipher them.

The other great trade at this time was in wreaths made with holly and berries. In mother's day the frames of the wreaths were made from straw, and she was still expert at binding a perfect circle in this way. Now wire frames were used, and these were padded with sphagnum moss which grew in the bogs of the Pentland hills and was sold round the shops by the sackful by hawkers. Mother would relate how, during the war, she had gathered this moss to be sent away, dried and cleaned, to be used as wound dressings in the military hospitals.

We bound the moss onto the iron frames with garden twine and then laid the holly flat, each spray overlapping, along the frame. First of all, however, we took off the holly berries, for it is best to use these to maximum effect. We used artificial berries too. There were two of these, one at each end of a short wire, and we used six in all twisted round a stiff wire and stuck into the frame.

The dexterity I showed in making wreaths no doubt helped to confirm Uncle Jim in his plans to acquire the McVeighs and he started, for the first time in all mother's widowhood, to visit us regularly.

Norah had already left school despite the pleas of the Rector of the Academy, and she was delivering fruit

195

and vegetables and helping in the shop of the mean couple who had drippy noses. Uncle Jim offered her a job with him which had, of course, "prospects". Working-class children were forever taking jobs with low wages and "prospects" never realised or even defined.

Soon Uncle Jim was pointing out that Norah had to pay train fares from Edinburgh every day, and when Mollie left school, as she soon would do, he could employ her as well but she also would have to pay tram and train fares. He would be moving to a new bungalow in the suburbs and grandfather's big house would be standing almost empty. Mother could look after her parents and live in comfort rent-free. He would see that I would get a good education at one of the "better" schools in Edinburgh and there would be "prospects" in the city for the whole family.

Eventually, partly because he had convinced mother that it was a good idea but mainly because she had such a strong sense of love and duty towards her parents, mother agreed to leave our home.

With our move to Edinburgh my story must end for, on leaving the village, the days of my childhood were all but over. Within less than a couple of years I was to be out on my own in the world, earning my living and looking after myself, even to cooking my own food. The years of childhood, for a time at least, would seem far away.

Mother's own tragedy proved to be continuous. When she got to Edinburgh she soon found that grandfather's house was mortgaged up to the hilt.

They had no money, and from that big house she had to go out charring in the houses around. Once more there was no one to help or to care and soon grandmother died, swiftly to be followed by grandfather, and soon after that mother had to leave that debt-ridden house for a weary succession of jobs with "accommodation" of one sort or another provided.

"Look after the bairns, Ella", father had said as he died. "Look after the bairns." For my gentle mother alone in her poverty, I can still only guess at her suffering in that long, weary battle. Somehow or other, and after a fashion, it was a battle she won, though she was not to live long enough to see the victory.

ISIS publish a wide range of books in large print, from fiction to biography. Any suggestions for books you would like to see in large print or audio are always welcome. Please send to the Editorial Department at:

ISIS Publishing Ltd.
7 Centremead
Osney Mead
Oxford OX2 0ES
(01865) 250 333

A full list of titles is available free of charge from:
Ulverscroft Large Print Books

(UK)
The Green
Bradgate Road, Anstey
Leicester LE7 7FU
Tel: (0116) 236 4325

(Australia)
P.O. Box 953
Crows Nest
NSW 1585
Tel: (02) 9436 2622

(USA)
1881 Ridge Road
P.O. Box 1230, West Seneca,
N.Y. 14224-1230
Tel: (716) 674 4270

(Canada)
P.O. Box 80038
Burlington
Ontario L7L 6B1
Tel: (905) 637 8734

(New Zealand)
P.O. Box 456
Feilding
Tel: (06) 323 6828

Details of **ISIS** complete and unabridged audio books are also available from these offices. Alternatively, contact your local library for details of their collection of **ISIS** large print and unabridged audio books.